INTELLIGENCE AND THE BRAIN

INTELLIGENCE AND THE BRAIN

Solving the Mystery of Why People Differ in IQ and
How a Child Can Be a Genius

Dennis Garlick, Ph.D.

AESOP
Press

First Edition

Grateful acknowledgement is made for the use of Figure 2, reprinted with permission from Cattell, 1987, *Intelligence: Its structure, growth and action,* p. 206. Copyright Elsevier Science Publishers.

Publisher's Cataloging-in-Publication Data

Garlick, Dennis.
    Intelligence and the brain : solving the mystery of
  why people differ in IQ and how a child can be a genius
  / Dennis Garlick. – 1st ed.
        p.   cm.
    Includes bibliographical references and index.
    ISBN-13: 978-0-615-31921-6
    ISBN-10: 0-615-31921-1
    1. Brain. 2. Intellect. 3. Intelligence levels. I. Title.
  QP398.G37 2010
  612.8'2   2009910548

www.intelligenceandthebrain.com
AESOP Press
Burbank, California

Printed in the United States of America

10 9 8 7 6 5 4 3 2 1

For Sherina

CONTENTS

PREFACE

I hope that this book will succeed in providing a new and convincing explanation of human intelligence. It will show how the environment is crucial for developing intelligence, but the genes cannot be ignored. Hopefully, it will enable us to finally turn the corner, providing a resolution to the nature/nurture debate that most can accept. However, while even experts in intelligence will find the contents of this book new, I have written it not for them but for a general audience. Why have I done this?

Partly it is because I did not want some journalist reading a more academic account of this approach and then popularizing it—both distorting the message and earning money for doing so (it is, after all, an explanation that I have been working on since early childhood). However, it is more than that. We will see that up until now, psychology has failed to explain intelligence because some of the most basic assumptions made by psychology are wrong. Only by rejecting these assumptions can serious progress be made in understanding human intelligence.

Since the topic of intelligence is controversial, I have tried to write this book so that readers can judge the evidence for themselves. Footnotes contain relevant references to the scientific literature, as well as additional comments that would likely be of more interest to academic readers. For the scientific references, I have typically chosen classic references rather than the most recent. This gives recognition to the original researchers, and also gives readers an indication of the timeline over which the relevant scientific advances have been made.

One assumption made by this book is that human intelligence is due to a biological process. Hence, while it is tempting to think that the mind can achieve anything because it is less tangible, the reality is not that simple. Just as biology places physical limits on us such as an inability to jump 100 feet in the air, biology also places limits on our intelligence. This is easily illustrated when someone is asked to do well on an IQ test, solve a complex mathematical problem, or predict the likely outcome in a novel situation. Only by understanding how biology determines intelligence can differences in intelligence be reduced.

Some also make the assumption that anyone interested in IQ has racist beliefs. However, this is far from true. I have written this book because I would like to see differences in intelligence reduced not just across people, but across race as well. Only by understanding IQ may this be achieved.

Unfortunately, due to the sensitivity of the IQ debate, it has meant that there is a lack of researchers and financial resources available at present. This has meant that studies that would shed further light on these issues are unable to be performed. Please contact me if you can provide funding, or are a researcher interested in these issues. Only with greater resources can further progress may be made.

I would especially like to thank those who took the time to read the entire manuscript and give detailed comments, including Arthur Jensen, Thomas Bouchard Jr., and James Stigler. Also thanks to various anonymous reviewers over the years, as well as others who have commented on parts of the manuscript. Finally, thanks to Aaron Blaisdell for giving me the time needed to write this book.

INTRODUCTION

Let us begin with what should be a simple question: What *is* intelligence? Is it simply the memorization of a lot of facts? Is it an innate ability that limits your potential? Is it something that people can learn at any age? Each of these is a popular belief, and books have been written advocating each of them. Still more books will dismiss the concept of IQ in a sentence or two, claiming that it does not really exist or is not important. The truth is that none of these views are correct.

Despite continual attempts to debunk IQ, the reality is that IQ continues to be a part of our society. Some of the most common banner ads on the internet purport to measure IQ—"Take the Dumb Test!" or "Albert Einstein had an IQ of 160. What's yours?"[1] People clicking on these ads suggests that there is still recognition of the relevance of IQ. Indeed, all parents would like their children to be gifted, and they invest billions of dollars each year hoping to give their children an intellectual advantage. Performance on IQ tests and college admission tests are still used to make important decisions when it comes to higher education and possible career paths. A defendant's IQ can also be used to determine their sentence in a criminal case. All of these factors suggest that there is a real need to understand what it is that IQ tests measure.

More importantly, ignoring differences in intelligence does not help children who are struggling at school. Indeed, one of the major messages of this book is that differences in intelligence are likely to be amplified by pretending that differences in intelligence do not exist. Differences in intelligence are also still readily apparent despite the many books claiming to be able to "make your child a genius" or "accelerate your mind." If these books were successful, then everyone would now be measuring at the genius level on IQ tests. However, the reality is that this is not happening. Many people still find IQ tests to be very challenging.

DIFFERENCES IN INTELLIGENCE AS A POLITICAL ISSUE

Beyond the existence of differences in intelligence, the possibility that these differences may be inherited is not a popular one. It would be much fairer if differences in intelligence were due to environmental factors. This would suggest that differences in intelligence could be eliminated through environmental interventions. However, we need to be very careful in attributing differences in intelligence to the environment, as this can be inflammatory.

For instance, imagine two children from the same school who show different levels of performance on an IQ test. If differences in intelligence are argued to be completely due to the environment, then this implies that they are under our control. Who then is to blame for the discrepancy in IQ? Is it the lower-IQ child for simply not working as hard in school as the higher-IQ child? Or is it the teachers for showing bias towards the higher-IQ student? Or are the parents of the lower-IQ child at fault for not having provided their child with the appropriate environment? On the other hand, if differences in intelligence are determined by the genes, this means that no one is to blame for differences in IQ performance.

Beyond the political controversies of the intelligence debate, every person has equal value in the world, irrespective of how they may score on an IQ test. It is the duty of society to ensure the well-being and happiness of everyone.

This book also makes no claim as to the importance of IQ relative to other abilities, talents, and skills. Howard Gardner is a Professor of Education at Harvard University and the founder of the theory of "multiple intelligences."[2] He believes that intelligence exists across a spectrum. This includes linguistic, logical-mathematical, spatial, bodily-kinesthetic, musical, interpersonal, and intrapersonal skills. IQ is unlikely to play a role in many of these abilities. Future success is also determined by other factors, including perseverance and responsibility. However, the importance of these other factors does not mean that IQ should be completely ignored. Only by understanding what underlies IQ can the effects of IQ be most successfully understood and addressed.

CURRENT DEFINITIONS OF INTELLIGENCE

Let us start by considering what we mean by the term *intelligence*. Even the definition of intelligence has been controversial.

Alfred Binet and Theodore Simon developed the original IQ test at the beginning of the twentieth century. They developed it to help children who were struggling at school by identifying those who needed remedial education. Identifying these children can be problematic, as the teacher's assessments of a child's potential can be biased by factors unrelated to that potential.

For example, a child might be exceptionally bright, but also very shy. Teachers might think that the child is not coping with the schoolwork because of the child's reluctance to answer questions. An IQ test can reveal that the child is indeed bright, and that it is their shyness that needs attention. Putting the child into a remedial class would be inappropriate in this case and would stunt the child's future development.

Another child might be having difficulty with schoolwork, but hides it by causing trouble in class. Identifying the difficulties with schoolwork means that the child's education can be adjusted to reflect their difficulties. This can help them to gain confidence and achieve success.

When it came to defining intelligence, Binet and Simon wrote that, "It seems to us that in intelligence there is a fundamental faculty, the alteration or the lack of which, is of the utmost importance for practical life. This faculty is judgment, otherwise called good sense, practical sense, initiative, the faculty of adapting one's self to circumstances."[3]

In 1944, David Wechsler developed another IQ test that is the most widely used IQ test today. It is known as the Wechsler Adult Intelligence

Scale (WAIS). There is also a version for children, known as the Wechsler Intelligence Scale for Children (WISC), and a version for very young children, known as the Wechsler Preschool and Primary Scale of Intelligence (WPPSI). Wechsler defined intelligence as "... the aggregate or global capacity of the individual to act purposefully, to think rationally, and to deal effectively with his environment."[4]

Arthur Jensen has written several prominent books on intelligence. In his 1980 book on *Bias in Mental Testing*, he defined intelligence as "the g factor of an indefinitely large and varied battery of mental tests," where the g factor refers to the observation that people who do well on one mental test also tend to do well on other mental tests.[5]

In 1994, Richard Herrnstein and Charles Murray published *The Bell Curve*.[6] This best-selling book engendered great controversy because it claimed that IQ was a better predictor of positive outcomes such as financial income and job success than factors like education or socioeconomic status. It also claimed that IQ was substantially inherited, and that race differences in IQ were also partly inherited.

In response to this controversy, fifty-two intelligence experts put forward a statement listing what is scientifically known about intelligence. They wrote that "Intelligence is a very general mental capability that, among other things, involves the ability to reason, plan, solve problems, think abstractly, comprehend complex ideas, learn quickly and learn from experience. It is not merely book learning, a narrow academic skill, or test-taking smarts. Rather, it reflects a broader and deeper capability for comprehending our surroundings—'catching on,' 'making sense' of things, or 'figuring out' what to do."[7]

Robert Sternberg is another iconic figure in the field of intelligence. He typically divides intelligence into three parts: analytic, creative, and practical. When asked to define intelligence, he says that it is "a mental activity directed toward purposive adaptation to, selection and shaping of, real-world environments relevant to one's life."[8]

Howard Gardner, who was mentioned earlier, is an advocate of "multiple intelligences." Of the term *intelligence* itself, he writes, "I balk at the unwarranted assumption that certain human abilities can be arbitrarily singled out as intelligence while others cannot."[9] He goes on to define intelligence as "the ability or set of abilities that allows a person to solve a problem or create a product that is of value in one or more cultures."[10]

These definitions indicate that the characterization of intelligence has grown broader over time. This has likely been related to the controversy and political issues surrounding the concept of intelligence. After all, the more characteristics that are included in *intelligence*, the more likely it is that everyone will have at least some of these characteristics.

However, this broadening of the definition also means that the term intelligence has lost a lot of its meaning. If intelligence is taken to represent almost any behavior, then how can we meaningfully evaluate such questions as the role of the genes and the environment in determining intelligence? Or what in the brain leads to differences in intelligence? With so many different behaviors encompassed by modern definitions of intelligence, narrowing down mechanisms and causes becomes practically impossible.

At the same time, it is clear that the definitions typically have in common the notion of better adaptation to the environnment or culture. In short, more intelligent people are better at predicting and reacting to the environment. As we will see, appreciating this characteristic becomes central if we are to understand human intelligence.

RECENT ADVANCES IN BRAIN SCIENCE

At the time IQ tests were developed, little was known about how the brain functioned. While theories of human intelligence have changed little since this time, major advances in our understanding of the brain have been made over the last few decades. These advances show that traditional theories of intelligence are not valid, and a new approach is needed based on what is now known about the brain and its development.

This book will begin by challenging some of the most basic assumptions that are made about intelligence. It will then show how the recent advances in the brain sciences can be used to provide a better understanding of intelligence. This integration will be shown to have major implications for many current beliefs concerning the nature of human intelligence. Finally, the implications of this for childhood education will be described.

CHAPTER ONE

A SURPRISINGLY NEW DEFINITION OF INTELLIGENCE: THE ABILITY TO UNDERSTAND

How might we better understand intelligence? Let us begin by going back to basics—to the original issue that prompted all of this debate about intelligence in the first place. When we go to a school, we will see that all the children in a class are not doing equally well. Children also know this. If we ask them, "Who is the smartest kid in the class?" they are not going to respond with answers like, "You cannot define intelligence, much less measure it," or "Intelligence is multifaceted and cannot be ranked on a single dimension." They will simply say that "John" or "Mary" is the smartest kid in the class.

So what is this based on? It is partly based on tests used at school. On these tests, "John" may consistently get marks close to 100% while

"David" may consistently get marks that are near the bottom of the class.

However, this is not getting at the underlying basis of intelligence. While children perform better or worse on tests, this is an outcome of differences in intelligence, not intelligence itself. A good teacher will know how the students are going to do before handing the test out, even if they have not given out any tests to these students before.

How does the teacher then know which students are going to do well on the test? In short, when the teacher instructs the class, "John" *understands* the material that the teacher is teaching. In other words, the bright students are the students that "get it." They then use this understanding to determine the correct answers on the tests. On the other hand, some students will often have difficulty understanding what the teacher is teaching. When the teacher explains something, they might be able to memorize the exact words the teacher uses. However, they will not be able to describe the concept using different words, or apply it to a new situation such as on a test. In short, despite being given the same explanation, some students are less able to *understand* it.[11]

This difference in the ability to understand is just as evident in college-age students. Despite the unfairness of it, any professor knows that some students in class will be "better" than others. By "better," we mean that the professor knows that he or she will present a complex argument only once, and the better student will immediately "get it." These students are also the ones who are most likely to get an "A" in the class. On the other hand, there are students who will really struggle to understand the material in the course. Even though they are working just as hard as the "A" students, they need to put all of this work in just to get a "C" and pass the course.

This equating of intelligence with the ability to understand is not controversial. The first definition of intelligence in the Oxford English Dictionary says that intelligence is the "faculty of understanding." So saying that intelligence is about understanding is straightforward and intuitive.

Differences in the Ability to Understand

The critical question then is—*why* are there these differences in the ability to understand? Why can some children understand the material presented in school more easily than others?

We can then see that the definitions of intelligence listed above are really missing the point. Sure, there is more to success in life than doing well in school. However, broadening the definition of intelligence to include other characteristics does not help us to achieve what we originally set out to do—namely explain why it is that some children find schoolwork easier than others.

To begin to answer this question about understanding, we need to consider what it is that makes something difficult to understand. Fortunately, there is widespread agreement on this account. To put it simply, something becomes more difficult to understand the more "abstract" it is. Both children and adults can very easily understand concrete concepts such as an instruction to eat an apple or to kick a ball. On the other hand, if an instruction involves a more abstract meaning, understanding is much more of a challenge.

Indeed, a well-known survey of 661 intelligence researchers found that 99.3% of respondents believed that "abstract thinking or reasoning" was central to intelligence, more than any other characteristic.[12] Further, psychologists who study childhood development have long known that as children get older, their ability to understand abstractions increases.[13] For instance, you can have a meaningful discussion with many adults about the concept of "liberty", but not with young children. This tells us that if we are to understand why some children find understanding more difficult, we really need to understand *abstraction*.

THE CHECKERED HISTORY OF PSYCHOLOGY

Unfortunately though, you might be surprised to hear that psychology tells us little about what it means to understand. In order to appreciate this, you need to know a bit about the history of psychology.

When psychology—or the scientific study of behavior—began back in the 1800s, it was very much concerned with the subjective experience of thinking.[14] When we think, what is happening in our mind? How do mental images lead to decision making? Introspection was used to describe one's own thoughts, and it was hoped that this would lead to an explanation of human behavior.

However, it was subsequently recognized that there was a major problem with this approach—there was no way to objectively verify people's reports of what they claimed they were thinking. You only had their word for it. This lack of corroboration made it difficult to determine exactly what was occurring in a person's mind. Because of this problem, psychology then turned around and completely rejected subjective experience or introspective reports as saying anything useful about the brain.

Instead, psychology chose to assess characteristics that could be corroborated by other means. This included stimuli that were presented to a person, and the person's actual behavior in response to these stimuli. Stimuli and behavior were considered to be more scientifically acceptable to study as they could be observed by multiple people, including those not directly involved in the situation. On the other hand, it was considered that subjective experiences such as someone *understanding* or "seeing" an explanation should be ignored.

Astute readers might now be thinking that psychology fails to explain a central part of human experience. However, it also tells us why psychology has had such a hard time providing an explanation of intelligence. In order to explain intelligence, you need to understand what it means to *understand*—but psychology has argued that this is a characteristic of thinking that should be ignored. So effectively, psychology can look at the outcome of intelligence in terms of behavior, but not actually understand what is going on in the mind to produce or explain this behavior.

Therefore, in contrast to typical psychological approaches, this book *is* about the capacity to understand. Why are there differences in the ability to understand abstractions? What causes these differences? Are these differences due to genes or the environment? How can a child's ability to understand abstractions be increased?

SO WHAT ARE ABSTRACTIONS?

Even though there is widespread agreement that abstraction is central to human intelligence, defining what abstraction means can be difficult. Indeed, when one looks in the dictionary for the definition of abstraction, a common definition is, literally, "not a concrete instance." This is almost like the old joke, "What is a cat?" Answer—"Not a dog!"

Such a definition does not help us to understand what abstraction is. Abstractions are quite often entities that people recognize, but it can be exceedingly difficult to define exactly *why* they are abstractions. So the first challenge to understanding intelligence is to define exactly what abstractions are. It turns out that abstractions have two key properties or characteristics.

First, abstractions actually represent a *reduction* in information. In other words, an abstraction contains less information than a concrete instance. The easiest way to illustrate this is to consider what is involved when you are asked to give a concrete example of an abstract concept. For instance, numbers are an example of abstraction. To give a concrete example, you add information or increase the number of details. To give a concrete instance of the number "three", you would say that there are three apples—the presence of the fruit is not necessary for the abstraction, but the presence of the fruit is necessary to give a concrete or real world example of the abstraction.

This reduction of information with abstraction is striking as it is often assumed that having more information is always better. However, a key point of abstraction is that it involves removing information.

This then raises the point about what information is eliminated, and what information is retained. This leads us to the second property of abstractions.

Second, abstractions represent information that is *consistent* or *in common* across situations. Essentially, abstractions are general principles that can be applied across different concrete situations or examples. This can be illustrated by the fact that you can give a number of different concrete examples of a given abstraction. Going back to the example of number, one concrete example of "three" is three apples. Another

14

concrete example of "three" is three pencils. Indeed, countless concrete examples could be given to illustrate the abstraction.

This characteristic of abstraction is also illustrated by how you would communicate an abstraction to someone when you do not have the language or a symbol to represent it. Imagine if you want to communicate the abstract concept of "three" to someone who speaks another language and does not know what the English word "three" means. If you showed the person three apples and said that this means "three," they would likely think that "three" means "apples."

How would you then communicate the abstract concept and not the concrete situation? You would communicate the concept of "three" by showing them three apples and saying "three," followed by three pencils and saying "three," followed by three books and again saying "three." Assuming that they understand the concept of "three," they would then realize that what you are trying to communicate is what is in common across these situations—namely the abstract number.

Abstractions, then, are the "essence" of a commonality across situations, stripped of the information that applies only to a particular concrete instance or example of the abstraction. This is quite intuitive. When you think of an abstraction or picture it in your mind, you will have a sense of what is in common across different examples of the abstraction without any details that are characteristic of a specific concrete instance. Consider examples like "three," "greater than," and "pumping." You are essentially seeing in your mind's eye the essence of the abstraction that can then fit across different concrete instances. As we will see later, appreciating these characteristics of abstraction are essential if we are to understand how the brain is able to identify abstractions.

WHY ARE ABSTRACTIONS IMPORTANT?

We often take our environment for granted. This means that we tend to not appreciate characteristics of our environment that enable us to be intelligent.

For instance, we often think that both our visual and auditory experiences are quite random. When someone is asked to give an example of a random visual environment, they will say something like "a page of text with all of the letters rearranged." When someone is asked to give an example of a random auditory environment, they might say "standing on a downtown street corner at lunch time."

However, both of these environments are by no means random. A truly random environment is one where any element is completely unrelated to, or independent of, every other element in the environment—there are no consistent patterns.

An old-style television tuned to a missing television station can show this. The screen will be full of "snow," and the speakers will be emitting "static." Newer televisions typically blank out this signal, but I am sure we have all seen it at one time or another.

The signal is random because the television is actually picking up many different signals from many different sources. These sources are independent of each other, so what one source is doing is not related to what the other sources are doing. This means that even though you know that one particular point on the screen is black or white at a given point in time, this does not tell you anything about whether another point on the screen will be black or white at the same time. All of the points are randomly determined, or independent of each other. Similarly, the static that emerges from the speakers is also due to many signals being received that are unrelated to each other. There is no pattern or consistency to the sound.

The important point to note here is that the environment we usually experience is not random like this.

Take the example of letters scrambled on a page. These letters represent elements that are tied together and repeated across the page. They are also the same combinations of elements that we typically see repeated all the time in our lives, such as in books and on road signs.

Similarly, standing on a downtown street corner at lunch time and listening will reveal many sounds that are repeated again and again. If two different people are talking, their voices will differ, and maybe even their accents. However, there is also a lot of commonality in terms of how different people pronounce their words. It is this commonality, across different speakers, which allows us to detect the same word being spoken by different speakers. This is true even though the sounds produced, such as by a man and a woman, may be quite different in many other respects.

Living in an Environment Made Up of Abstractions

It is this lack of randomness in our world that makes intelligence possible. If the environment was truly random, then experience with an event in the past could not be used to predict the same event in the future. Throwing a ball the same way may lead to it going up, down, left, or right on different occasions, without any way to predict what will occur the next time the ball is thrown. Fortunately, our environment does have repeatability. The exact same conditions are likely to lead to the same outcome at different points in time.

However, our environment has more than consistency from one event to another. Many events follow similar rules or general principles. This means that the outcome will be the same, irrespective of other characteristics that are present. Knowledge of these general principles may then be used to predict outcomes.

As an example, gravity ensures that objects will typically fall down towards the ground if they are not supported. This underlying principle can then be used to predict specific events that we do not have actual experience of. For instance, what would happen if you threw a diamond ring up in the air? Few people have done this because a diamond ring tends to be valuable, but we do not need to do it to know what will happen. It can be predicted that the ring will fall back to the ground, as the ring will behave like other objects that fall to the ground because of their mass. It does not matter that the ring is a different color or shape to other objects that we have thrown in the air. We know that these characteristics are irrelevant in predicting what the ring will do.

This is just one example of general patterns in the environment that predict the likely outcome of events. Terms used to describe abstractions such as "half", "diffusion", "threshold", and "liberty" all refer to consistencies or similarities across events. We are surrounded with general principles like these.

The Advantage of Abstractions

By identifying and understanding these general principles, similarities between previously experienced events and new events can be recognized. This enables knowledge of past events to be used to make correct predictions about new situations.

Without this knowledge, experience with the exact same situation in the past would be needed to know what the current outcome will be. However, this is problematic, as it is often not possible to have had experience with the exact same situation before. There are many concrete situations for every abstraction. Further, even if all of the possible concrete situations can be experienced and remembered, often you would like to be able to predict an outcome. This can help to avoid undesirable outcomes rather than having to experience them initially so that you can know what will happen in the future.

Knowing the correct behavior to perform without trial and error can also be advantageous even if you are not harmed for producing a wrong behavior. There is the old fable that a million monkeys typing for a million years would eventually recreate the works of Shakespeare. While this may be true, typically we want to produce the correct behavior to achieve a desirable outcome in a much shorter period than a million years. There can be an astronomical number of different behaviors that can be exhibited in many situations. Trying out each and every behavior to get a desired outcome is impractical. By using understanding, this can guide our behavior and more quickly lead to success.

This indicates that intelligence is based on the nature of our environment. In a random environment, such as predicting the outcome of a dice roll, an intelligent person will be no different to an unintelligent person in predicting the outcome—as the outcome is truly random. However, in many cases, underlying patterns or abstractions mean that an outcome is not random. By being aware of abstractions that are present in the environment, knowledge from one situation can be used to make predictions about the likely outcomes of other situations. In this way, people who understand abstractions are able to perform correctly in many more situations than would be expected based on their direct concrete experience alone.

And note the importance of the environment here. Abstractions are fundamentally about understanding the *environment*.

UNDERSTANDING OF ABSTRACTIONS IS A CHALLENGE

When we talk about perceiving abstractions, we can also observe that perception of them would initially seem to be easy. If different people say the same letter to you, such as "A," you immediately recognize that they are saying the same thing. You also immediately recognize the letter "A" if you see it typed in a book, written in freehand by a person, or on a road sign at night. Perception of such abstractions seems to occur quickly and automatically—there is no need to think about how you do them.

In fact, often we cannot even define or consciously say what constitutes a particular abstraction. For instance, what are the exact sounds that distinguish the letter "A" from the letter "E?" Rather, the abstraction just seems to pop into our head when we are exposed to a concrete example of it. Arguably the most frustrating aspect of explaining something to someone who cannot understand an abstraction is that when you can understand it, the abstraction seems obvious. If it makes sense in your own head, it is hard to understand why others do not just "get it."

However, a major argument of this book is that even though the perception of abstractions seems obvious and effortless, perceiving abstractions is actually a major computational challenge.[15]

In the case of speech recognition, your ears are presented with numerous inputs representing information about the pitch and amplitude of the incoming sound. Some information, such as the sound of a car engine in the distance, is completely irrelevant. Even much of the information from the person's voice is also irrelevant. Men and women sound quite different, as do people from different language backgrounds and different geographical regions. Even two adults of the same sex and age will frequently have very different sounding voices—this is how we are able to recognize who is speaking by hearing their voice alone. Despite all of these differences, when different people say the same letter, we are able to recognize the letter as being the *same*.

Visual perception is just as challenging. When a word is presented in different contexts, the text may be a different size, the font may be different, and the color of the text and the background may also differ. These differences do not affect our ability to perceive the word. Signwriters do not think, "We need to use white writing on a black background for the sign or people will not recognize the words!" When trying to read a sign, you do not need to walk a few feet closer or a few feet further away to read the text as the text needs to be a certain size to be understood. When presented with a word on a sign we can immediately read it, irrespective of these characteristics.

To use an example that is even simpler than words, simply identifying a shape such as a circle is in fact a major challenge. Depending on the size of the circle, different receptors in our eyes are activated. If the circle is drawn poorly, the curve will also not correspond to a true circle. Even if we can get around these differences, how do we focus on the circle and identify it when there is other information entering our eyes at the same time—such as the paper the circle is drawn on, the desk the paper is sitting on, and whatever other objects are on the desk at the same time?

Computers and Abstraction

This challenge of perception is perhaps best illustrated by attempts to program computers to perceive or understand information that would seem obvious to us.

In a classic example, Marvin Minsky, a celebrated artificial intelligence researcher, once asked a graduate student to program a computer over the summer to identify objects presented to it by a video camera. After all, how difficult is it to identify whether an object is an apple or a pencil? So getting a computer to do this should be a relatively simple task. However, when the student actually tried to do this, they found that it was exceedingly difficult and they never succeeded.

This is a striking example, as Marvin Minsky was a giant in the field of artificial intelligence at the time. His lack of understanding of the difficulty of perception suggested that researchers in artificial intelligence fundamentally misunderstood the complexity of what the brain seems to do automatically. Unfortunately, many theories of artificial intelligence have been based on these misunderstandings.

Indeed, books in the 1970s predicted that by the year 2000 we would all have our own personal robot maid. This maid would wander around the house serving food, doing the dishes, and making the beds. After all, a maid's work would seem to be quite simple to do. However, such technology is still not available, well after it was predicted to be commonplace. The reason that robot maids are not available is because they would need to be able to perceive objects so that they could pick them up or avoid them while moving. While we find these tasks simple, digital computers are still not able to perform them reliably. Similarly, everyone would like to be able to dictate messages to their computer so the computer can convert their voice to words on the screen. However, anyone who has tried speech recognition software knows that we are still a long way from attaining this goal.

These tasks—which humans perform every day—turn out to be exceedingly difficult to program into machines. Even examples of success are often based on different principles to those used by humans to solve the same problems.

For instance, major advances have been made in robot-controlled aircraft. However, these aircraft do not perceive their location based on visual landmarks in the way that we do when we navigate the environment. Instead, these aircraft rely on signals from both satellites and the ground to determine their own location and that of their goal or target. Mathematical equations are then used to calculate the correct trajectory to move from their current location to their goal. Collision avoidance in cars is not based on visual recognition of objects, but on the use of radar. The use of robots in assembly lines is based on the knowledge that the parts they are working on will be in precisely predetermined positions so that the robot can "know" where it is.

It follows, then, that if the perception of even simple abstractions is in fact a major challenge, the perception of more abstract concepts is even more of a challenge—one that many children and even some adults can find quite difficult. How can an abstract concept just pop into our head when we are exposed to it? More specifically, how can we "see" or "picture" it in our minds? How can we form a mental representation of the abstraction that is independent of the context, which then allows us to observe or apply it to other contexts as well? This seemingly simple process that we take for granted as adults is central to an understanding of human intelligence.

CHAPTER TWO

MEASURING
THE ABILITY TO UNDERSTAND

Measurement provides the bedrock upon which much of science is based. Sciences such as physics and chemistry rely on measurement to identify whether phenomena are related to each other or not, and to make predictions that may be confirmed by experiments.

In the case of understanding, measuring can give us information such as whether the ability to understand changes as people age. If understanding does change, this suggests that if we want to know what in the brain is responsible for understanding, we should look for something in the brain that is changing over the same time.

Tests That Measure Understanding

Psychologists have developed numerous tests that measure the ability to understand abstractions.[16] Three tests that are commonly used are Raven's Progressive Matrices, Word Analogies, and Number Series. These are illustrated in Figure 1. Many readers will have been given tests like these during their schooling or when being assessed in the workplace. It is instructive to look at these tests in detail if we are to understand how psychologists attempt to measure intelligence.

Raven's Progressive Matrices

In Raven's Progressive Matrices, examinees are required to identify which of the elements at the bottom should go in the space above to complete the main figure. To do this, they need to observe the relationships that are applied across the rows and columns, and then apply these relationships to the final row and column to determine the missing element that is consistent with the other elements.

For example, in the first example, they are mirror images, or create a square—so the answer would be A.

In the second item, the number of elements is increasing by one element as you go across the row, even though the orientation of the elements is different. As you go down the column, the elements are rotating counterclockwise, irrespective of the number of elements. This indicates that for the final element, you should choose one that has three elements, and the elements should be rotated so that they are horizontal. Another way of solving the second item is to go across the rows and notice that the number of elements is increasing, while the orientation stays the same. Either way, the correct answer would be C.

Raven's Progressive Matrices

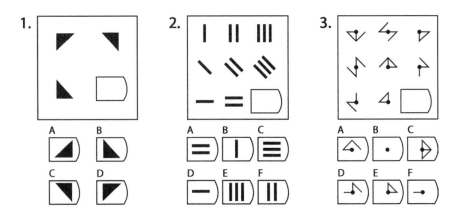

Word Analogies

1. Puppy is to Dog, as Kitten is to *Cat*

2. Girder is to Skyscraper, as Bone is to *Body*

3. Vindicative is to Revenge, as Mercenary is to *Money*

Number Series

1.   2 4 6 8 *10*

2.   44 45 47 51 58 *69*

3.   40 32 57 34 69 37 77 43 82 54 *85*

Figure 1. Tests used by psychologists that measure the ability to understand abstractions.

The correct answer for the third item is given in the endnotes.[17] If you are having difficulty with it, here is a hint—you need to treat each individual line as an abstraction, or independent of its context.

Word Analogies

In Word Analogies, the first two words are related by an abstraction. You then need to apply this abstraction to the third word, determining the word that would complete the abstraction so it is the same abstraction as it was for the first two words.

For example, in the first item, a Puppy is a young version of a Dog. However, "young version" is not a concept that applies just to puppies and dogs. It is an abstraction that applies across many concrete examples, including the relationship between a Kitten and a Cat. So if you understand the abstraction and are prompted with Kitten, you will produce the answer *Cat*.

In the second item, a Girder is the structure contained within a Skyscraper that allows it to stay upright and resist gravity. This is the same function that Bones fulfill in the Body, so the correct answer would be *Body*. Again we can see that the abstraction applies across the different concrete instances, and we need to understand the abstraction to answer the problem correctly.

The third item is again more difficult. It illustrates how the abstraction in common across items is often not easy to perceive or understand.

Number Series

In Number Series, you need to give the next number in a series that preserves the general pattern. Again this involves applying a general principle or abstraction to determine the answer.

In the first item, the numbers are produced by adding a common amount, namely 2, to each element. To get the next number in the series, you need to repeat this general principle of adding 2 to the final number, 8, giving you the correct answer of 10.

The second item is more complicated. The differences between the numbers going from left to right are 1, 2, 4, and 7. The differences between these differences are 1, 2, and 3. Applying the same consistent process, the difference between the final number and the answer needs to be 7 + 4 = 11. Hence, the answer is 58 + 11 = 69.

The third item involves appreciating that there are two separate general principles that are determining the numbers. The appropriate general principle needs to be identified and applied to determine the correct answer. Again, the Number Series items involve identifying general principles that are applied across different concrete instances.

THESE TESTS DEPEND ON UNDERSTANDING ABSTRACTIONS

Despite differences in content, we can see how abstractions are central to doing well on each of these tests. These abstractions also fit the criteria for abstraction that we described earlier. In particular, each of the problems involve a situation where there is something in common or the same across the elements. At the same time, each element is not exactly the same—they each have a context or specific details that vary from one element to the next. It is this context or specific details that distinguish the concrete instances from each other. The challenge is to identify the abstractions independent of their context.

These problems are also very like applying abstractions in real life. Often, we are presented with a situation where we have no prior experience. If we rely only on past concrete experience, we would not know what to do in the new situation. However, if we can identify an abstraction or commonality between this situation and another situation that we are familiar with, we can then use this abstraction to guide our behavior in the new situation. Assuming that the new situation does conform to the underlying general principle, our behavior in the new situation can still be successful.

This is confirmed by the finding that people who do well on the above tests that assess abstractions also do well in other situations that involve abstractions. This includes school and college courses, as well as occupations that involve producing solutions using abstractions or general principles.[18]

Of course, this does not mean that solving these problems requires only the understanding of abstractions. All of these problems also depend on at least some concrete knowledge. In Raven's Progressive Matrices, you need to be able to understand the instructions telling you that you should pick the element at the bottom that fits the pattern. In Word Analogies, you need to know what the words mean. In Number Series, you need to know basic arithmetic. However, having this concrete knowledge alone will not enable you to solve any of these problems. You need not only this concrete knowledge, but also to understand what is in common across the situations. Applying this understanding enables the problems to be solved.

Increasing performance on these tests is also exceedingly difficult. If a person gets one of these problems wrong, you can tell them what the correct answer is. You can even tell them how to work out the correct answer. However, if they are then given another problem based on the same abstractions, often they will not be able to solve the new problem. While they are able to memorize the solution to the original problem, they are unable to *understand* the abstraction and apply it to other similar problems. Again, while we tend to take the ability to understand abstractions for granted, understanding abstractions can be a great challenge.

ARE SOME PEOPLE BETTER AT UNDERSTANDING IN GENERAL?

Once we have tests that can be used to measure a person's ability to understand, we can see if people who are better at understanding some abstractions are better at understanding other abstractions as well.

Intuitively, we might predict that they are. It is known that children are often described as being "bright" or "gifted." If a child is classified in this way, they can enter advanced educational programs in many different subjects. This implies that a gifted child is good at understanding abstractions in many different domains. Similarly, if a parent is told that their child is gifted, the parent does not immediately ask—"What subject is my child gifted in?" Implicit in saying that a child is gifted is that the child is good at understanding many different school subjects.

This pattern is also observed when performance on the tests of understanding described earlier is examined. A child who is good at solving Raven's Progressive Matrices also tends to be good at solving Word Analogies and Number Series. In other words, children or adults who are good at one test of abstraction tend to be good at other tests of abstraction as well. This observation has been frequently documented.[19]

31

This would seem to be surprising. After all, the content involved in these three tests would seem to be very different. Raven's Progressive Matrices involves reasoning using figures, Word Analogies involves words or language, and Number Series involves numbers and arithmetic. The observation that children who are gifted tend to do well on all of these types of problems indicates that there is a general ability to understand abstractions. Those who are higher in this ability can do well at identifying or understanding abstractions in many different contexts or situations.

This finding is also the likely reason we use a single term "intelligence" to refer to the ability to understand abstractions. If the ability to understand abstractions was dependent on the content area, we would not talk about "intelligent" people. Instead, we might identify people as being "number" people, "language" people, or "spatial" people. Or maybe other types of people. Our language would represent the differences that are seen to occur in the world, in the same way that we do not use a single term to refer to both "anger" and "fear" since it is recognized that these are two different traits and someone can exhibit one and not necessarily the other.

This finding is also the reason that IQ tests use a single score to represent intelligence. An IQ test does not claim to comprehensively test all possible mental abilities. Instead, it uses a limited number of subtests to assess a sample of abilities. The notion is that while only a limited number of abilities are assessed, someone who does well on these subtests is likely to do well in other situations that involve other abstractions. Given the unpopularity of the idea of a single intelligence factor, IQ tests would have been abandoned long ago unless there was at least some validity to the IQ concept.

The educational system is also based on this characteristic. Performance on college admissions tests is used to determine places at college—even though college content is often different to what was assessed on the admission test. This is possible because performance at understanding some concepts such as those on the admission test provides an indicator of how well someone will be able to understand other concepts such as those at college.

For instance, you know that a doctor may never have been assessed on his ability to understand a certain physiological test before becoming a doctor. However, you have confidence that he will be able to understand the physiological test as he has already demonstrated the ability to understand other complex abstractions. On the other hand, someone who does not understand basic mathematical or scientific principles is unlikely to be able to understand the same physiological test.

Opponents of this concept often respond with the claim that a school student can be, for example, good at Math but poor at English. However, this tends to be anecdotal, in that it generally refers to an individual who is believed to exhibit this characteristic. A single example does not contradict the finding that, in general, children who are good at understanding one content domain are often good at understanding other content domains as well.[20] In addition, if these cases are examined closely, it will often be found that the student who was good at Math but poor at English was actually quite good at English as well—just not as good as they were at Math. Individual interests need to be taken into account when looking at these cases as well. If the student can understand the material but does not find it interesting or enjoyable, they are less likely to work hard in the subject. If they do not work hard, then they will not get good marks, even if they are having little difficulty understanding the material. This is an important point that we will be returning to later—namely that intelligence only predicts potential, and may not be realized if the child does not put in substantial effort.

Of course, it would be easy to write a book that denies that people who are good at understanding some abstractions are also good at understanding other abstractions. This would be more popular. However, a book that genuinely wants to illuminate why there are differences in understanding abstractions cannot afford this luxury. Also, no strong claims are being made as to just how widespread this ability to understand abstractions is, or how important it is for future success. There are other domains and ways to be successful, and these depend on other talents that can be unrelated to the ability to understand abstractions. However, the reality is that understanding abstractions is important for school, college, and some occupations. Only by examining how differences in understanding manifest themselves can it be understood why differences in understanding exist, and how they may be reduced.

How Does the Ability to Understand Change with Age?

Once we have tests that measure a person's ability to understand abstractions, we can use these tests to examine whether the ability to understand abstractions improves as a person gets older. In short, as a person ages, are they able to answer more items on the tests correctly?

In Childhood

It is found that children's performance on the tests of abstraction improve as they get older. At the age of five, most children will have difficulty solving problems that involve more than the most basic of abstractions. At the age of ten, they will be able to understand some more difficult abstractions. By adulthood, they will be able to solve many more high-level abstraction problems. In short, as children get older, they get smarter. This should not be surprising. It is well known that there are certain things that you cannot explain to young children as they are too young to understand them. Also, as has already been noted, child psychologists have long known that as children become older, they are more able to understand abstractions.[21]

In Adulthood

What about understanding in adulthood? Intuitively, an astute reader might say that the ability to understand abstractions does not similarly increase in adulthood. A good example to illustrate this can be found in a public library. Here, there will be different sections for adult and children's books. Often, the children's book section is further divided by age group, such as young, middle, and teen sections. This is done because it is recognized that some books, such as those contained in the teen section, are too difficult for young readers to understand—the books are beyond their comprehension.

On the other hand, the adult section in the library is not divided into sections for twenty- to twenty-five-year-olds, twenty-five- to thirty-year-olds, etc. This is because there is a fundamental difference between intellectual development before and after maturity. Indeed, a bright twenty-year-old has the ability to understand any book in the library—even books written by eighty-year-olds. On the other hand, if a book is difficult to understand or beyond the comprehension of someone at age twenty, then it is likely that they will always have difficulty understanding the material. They will just accept that they were not cut out for this particular domain and will follow other interests.

Our education system is also based on the principle that the ability to understand changes during childhood but not adulthood. At around sixteen years of age, teenagers around the world are given a test that measures their ability to understand the material they were taught at school. This test determines their future career paths, such as whether college is an option for them.

If the ability to understand continued to increase, students would be able to retake these tests in later life and improve their score substantially. However, this is not what is found. People cannot do significantly better at these tests by re-sitting them in later adulthood. Even if older people sit the tests, they are not the top scorers, despite their many more years of experience.

College is also based on the principle that the ability to understand does not increase in adulthood. There are no courses that are considered to be so difficult to understand that students can only enroll in them once they are, for example, at least thirty years of age. It is accepted that once a person reaches adulthood, they will be as capable of understanding the material as adults of any age.

Consider also college professors. College professors may have been studying their field for decades. If the ability to understand continued to develop throughout life, then they would have accumulated an ability to understand many abstractions that would be well beyond any twenty-year-old. And yet, they do not view their students as mere "infants" who are incapable of understanding what they themselves can understand. Indeed, bright students will be able to understand any of the concepts that the professor talks about. Graduate students and post-doctoral researchers also make many major scientific advances and are considered to be equal to professors in their ability to understand—even though they may be twenty-five years of age or younger.

Outside of college, older adults do not think that a thirty-year-old, but not a twenty-year-old, will be able to understand an abstraction. This is in contrast to children, where it is recognized that age plays a large role in what someone is able to understand. Concepts need to be simplified if one is talking to children, even if the children are in their early teens. All of these observations suggest that while the ability to understand increases in childhood, it does not continue to increase in adulthood.

These intuitions are confirmed when adults are given the above tests that assess the ability to understand abstractions. It is found that adults do not improve on these tests as they get older—how a person does on these tests as a twenty-year-old is similar to how they will do as a thirty-year-old. Indeed, performance on these tests of understanding can actually decline in later adulthood. This should not come as a surprise to older adults. Many older adults will readily admit that they are less acute or bright at age forty than they were at age twenty—even though they were certainly better able to understand things at age twenty than they were at age five or ten.

Illustrating Performance on Intelligence Tests at Different Ages

Figure 2 shows graphically what is found by psychologists when intelligence tests are given to people of different ages. It confirms what we have talked about. The solid line illustrates performance on the tests we examined earlier that depend on abstractions for their solution. Psychologists often refer to these tests as measuring *fluid intelligence*. As the figure shows, performance on these tests is observed to improve over childhood—indicating that children are better able to understand abstractions as they get older. However, performance on these tests does not continue to

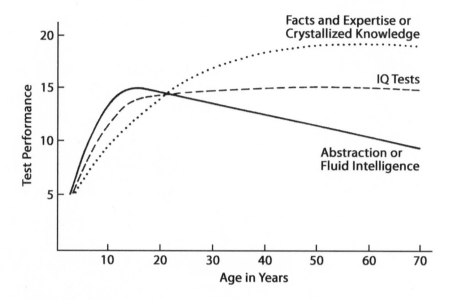

Figure 2. Performance on tests of abstraction (or fluid intelligence), facts and expertise (or crystallized knowledge), and IQ over the lifespan. Taken from Cattell, 1987, p. 206.

increase in adulthood as well. Performance peaks around the age of sixteen years, and then actually starts to decline in later life.[22]

The figure also shows a dotted line. This indicates performance on tests that involve recalling specific facts or general knowledge, such as "What is the capital of France?" and "What is a salamander?" These types of questions are common on television quiz shows such as Jeopardy and Sale of the Century. Psychologists use the term *crystallized knowledge* to refer to performance on these types of tests. As can be seen from the figure, performance on these tests increases not only in childhood, but during much of adulthood as well. This is again not surprising. It is well known that adults are able to memorize new facts for much of their life—leading to increased expertise.

The final line on the figure is a dashed line, which shows performance on traditional IQ tests. We will look at IQ tests in more detail later in this chapter. For now, we can see that performance on IQ tests improves over childhood, and stays about the same throughout adulthood. This is because IQ tests consist of subtests that assess both the ability to understand abstractions and crystallized knowledge.

In childhood, both the ability to understand abstractions and crystallized knowledge increase. Since IQ tests assess both of these characteristics, it follows that performance on IQ tests will increase during this time. In adulthood, the ability to understand abstractions decreases, while crystallized knowledge continues to increase. This means that an older adult's better crystallized knowledge can compensate for their worse performance using abstractions. Typically they do better on some IQ subtests and worse on others—resulting in their overall IQ score often not changing substantially as they age. This is consistent with the real-world observation that older adults may not be as mentally acute, but they compensate for this with greater knowledge and wisdom.

The pattern of performance shown in this figure is well established. It has been observed ever since intelligence tests were first administered to people over 100 years ago.[23]

HOW DO PEOPLE DIFFER IN THE ABILITY TO UNDERSTAND?

We have seen how the ability to understand abstractions increases over childhood. Why, then, do children differ in the ability to understand? Is it the case that some children are just more able to understand abstractions right from birth? Or is it that some children improve their ability to understand abstractions over childhood while others do not? Neither of these is true.

All children show the same behaviors when they are just born. They then gradually develop the ability to understand more and more abstractions as they get older—as we have already seen. However, children do not develop at the same rate. Some children develop faster than others. As they get older, they are better able to understand abstractions compared to other children of the same age. They learn to speak earlier, learn to read earlier, and can attend more advanced classes at school.

This means that different tests of understanding need to be used to identify giftedness at different ages. A test that is good for identifying differences in the ability to understand at a young age will not be effective at identifying giftedness at an older age. All of the older children will perform well on the younger-age test.

For instance, a young child may be identified as gifted by their ability to understand a word such as "uncle"—knowing that it refers not to a specific person, such as their own uncle, but to a general relationship such that an uncle is the brother of a person's mother or father. However, by high school, practically all children will understand the true meaning of the word "uncle." In order to identify a gifted child at this age, much more difficult tests need to be used, such as understanding the meaning of "fallacies" and being able to give a number of concrete examples of "fallacies."

Therefore, giftedness does not refer to a particular behavioral characteristic that is present from an early age and stays the same over childhood. Being gifted means that a child's ability to understand abstractions increases more quickly over childhood, relative to other children of the same age.

HOW DOES THIS RELATE TO IQ?

We have seen how the ability to understand abstractions increases over childhood. However, many who are familiar with IQ tests would know that a person's IQ is supposed to stay the *same* over childhood. For instance, a bright child might be said to have an IQ of 130, no matter what their age. Does this contradict the above findings showing that the ability to understand abstractions increases? It does not, but we need to look more closely at how IQ testing works to understand this.

IQ tests are like the other tests of intelligence, but typically consist of a number of subtests that assess different domains. Further, they can typically only be administered to one person at a time. This means that more can be observed about a person's performance than what is revealed by their answer alone. The IQ tester can observe how the person goes about answering a problem, and can also better assess the person's level of understanding by asking further questions based on the individual's initial responses.

However, despite these differences in administration, the subtests on IQ tests often assess the ability to understand abstractions. For instance, the *Comprehension* subtest involves understanding the general or abstract reasons behind situations. *Similarities* involves identifying what abstract principle is in common between two concrete objects, for example, "How are eggs and fish alike?" *Picture Arrangement* involves sorting pictures into an order that tells a story based on general themes that are commonly encountered in the environment. *Arithmetic* involves using general mathematical principles in a specific concrete situation to produce the correct answer. For example, "John bought four books for six dollars each. How much did he pay all together?"

So the IQ subtests are like the previous tests we examined that involve understanding abstractions for correct performance. However, the question remains; how does a person's IQ score tend to stay the same over childhood if their ability to understand abstractions is increasing?

Calculating IQ Scores

In order to understand IQ scores, we need to look at how they are calculated. IQ stands for *Intelligence Quotient*. Quotient means dividing one number by another. In the case of IQ, a person's score is determined by dividing their Mental Age by their Chronological Age, and then multiplying by 100.

Mental Age is defined as the age at which an average child exhibits a particular level of performance. In other words, how old is the typical child when they perform that well on the test? Chronological Age is how old the child actually is, or their biological age.

It follows that if a child performs at the same level as a typical child of their own age, then their Mental Age will be the same as their Chronological Age. Dividing one by the other, and then multiplying by 100, leads to an IQ of 100. For example, a twelve-year-old who performs like typical twelve-year-olds on the test will have an IQ of 12/12 x 100 = 100. An IQ of 100 represents the average IQ score.

If a child is gifted for their age, this means that they perform better than a typical child of the same age. They might perform like a typical child who is two years older. Hence, a twelve-year-old will then have a Mental Age of a fourteen-year-old. Their IQ will then be 14/12 x 100 = 116. An IQ score greater than 100 indicates that a child is doing better than other children of the same age.

More recent IQ tests use a procedure whereby a person's performance is directly compared to the performance of other people of the same age, often referred to as a normative sample. However, despite this difference in procedure, the underlying variations in intellectual performance are the same.[24]

We can see from this description that implicit in IQ scores is the notion that performance improves on the tests as children progress through childhood. Since a person's chronological age is continually increasing, this means that their IQ would go down if their mental age or performance on the IQ test stayed the same. IQ can only stay the same over childhood if mental performance is actually *increasing*.

This is reflected in the design of IQ tests. The problems that are used to identify gifted five-year-olds are quite easy, such that any adult would find them easy to answer. On the other hand, the problems that are used to identify gifted sixteen-year-olds are so difficult that many adults will struggle to solve them.

What, then, about adulthood? Previously, we reviewed evidence showing that the ability to understand abstractions does not increase in adulthood like it does in childhood. If this were true, you would initially expect an adult's IQ to decline over time. Their Mental Age remains constant, while their Chronological Age continues to increase. This is actually what originally happened when the IQ concept was first used to describe adult intelligence!

To fix this, the calculation of IQ was further tweaked. If a person was over sixteen years of age, their Chronological Age was fixed at sixteen when calculating their IQ score—irrespective of their real age. Therefore, the reason that IQ does not diminish in adulthood is because while a person's Mental Age does not change, their Chronological Age does not change either for the purpose of calculating their IQ.[25]

What IQ Tests Really Mean

The fact that differences in intelligence may be represented by IQ indicates that intellectual performance or the ability to understand abstractions increases over childhood, and that children also differ in the rate at which this occurs. This is illustrated by Figure 3, which shows what IQ tells us about how the ability to understand changes over the lifespan for people who are high, average, and low in IQ.[26]

As can be seen from the figure, IQ in no way indicates that intelligence is fixed over the lifespan. Both IQ tests and tests of abstraction indicate that the ability to understand abstractions increases over childhood. If we focus specifically on fluid intelligence or the ability to understand abstractions, the curves should show a decline in later adulthood.

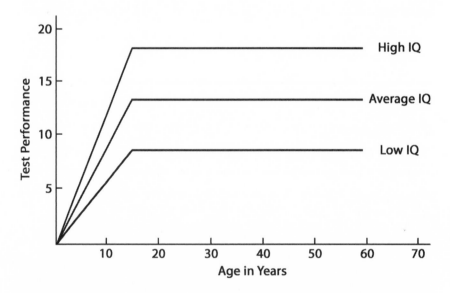

Figure 3. A simplified illustration of what IQ testing tells us about how performance on intelligence tests changes over the lifespan for people who differ in intelligence.

However, we are ignoring this to simplify the discussion. The important point is that the ability to understand abstractions does not continue to increase in adulthood like it does in childhood. The implication of this for childhood development will be a major focus of this book.

CHAPTER THREE

WHAT IQ TELLS US ABOUT THE ABILITY TO UNDERSTAND

This book is concerned with explaining what causes differences in the ability to understand abstractions. When we look at the research literature, we find that most research in intelligence has used IQ tests rather than tests that specifically focus on understanding abstractions. However, since the ability to understand abstractions is a major contributing factor to performing well on IQ tests, we can still use the outcomes of these studies to provide insight into the process responsible for understanding.

The Stability of IQ over the Lifespan

The first question we can ask is whether a person's IQ is stable over time. In other words, is someone who is good at understanding abstractions at one age likely to be good at understanding abstractions at another age?

We learned in the previous chapter that the ability to understand abstractions increases over childhood. A stable IQ throughout childhood indicates that a child's intellectual performance keeps improving sufficiently such that children with a lower IQ do not improve more rapidly and overtake them. In other words, the child's ranking relative to other children stays the same over childhood, while intellectual abilities are increasing for all children.

Studies examining the stability of IQ over time have found that IQ is surprisingly stable over childhood.[27] A person's IQ score at 8 years of age is likely to be closely related to their IQ score in adulthood. In fact, even a child's IQ at age 2 can be used to predict their IQ in adulthood—although it will not be as accurate a predictor as their IQ at later ages. IQ shows even more stablility in adulthood. These findings suggest that whatever it is that causes differences in IQ, it starts to operate from a young age, and its effect continues to influence intelligence throughout life.[28]

Examining the Contribution of Genes and Environment

In trying to determine the cause of differences in the ability to understand, we can next examine whether differences are due to the genes or the environment, otherwise known as nature versus nurture. Unfortunately, there are a number of common misconceptions in relation to estimating the contribution of genes and environment to human characteristics.

One claim is that human development is due to an interaction between the genes and the environment. Hence, it is claimed that it is nonsensical to talk about the independent contributions of either the genes or the environment to any human characteristic. It is said that they interact, and their effects cannot be independently separated.

However, such a claim does not take into account what is being investigated in scientific studies that look at the contribution of genes and environment. These studies are not concerned with whether the genes or the environment *cause* a particular characteristic. Clearly, both the genes and the environment are fundamentally important. Without the genes, an embryo would not have been present in the first place. Without the environment, the genes would not have received the necessary food for the embryo to grow into a child. So we can say that both the genes and the environment are *necessary* for a child to develop.

Despite this, we can still investigate whether the genes, the environment, or both, are responsible for *differences* in a characteristic across people.

A Music Analogy

To illustrate this, consider the analogy of a musician playing a violin concerto.[29] In this case, it is impossible to say whether the musician or the violin is responsible for the performance. Clearly, both contribute, and if you took away either, there would not be any music.

However, what if more than one concerto is performed and there are differences across the performances? We can then examine whether the musician or the violin is responsible for the differences.

Consider the case where the same musician plays the concerto twice using two different violins. One violin is a renowned Stradivarius, while the other is a cheap violin that is poorly tuned. You would expect that there would be big differences between the performances. However, you can also identify the cause—the violin.

In another case, two different musicians perform the concerto. One musician is highly accomplished, while the other has only recently begun lessons. They use the same violin. Again, there would be big differences in the performances. However, this time, it would be apparent that the cause of the difference was in the relative abilities of the musicians.

From this example, we can see that even though it is nonsensical to talk about the relative contributions of the musician and the violin to producing a specific concerto performance, it is quite meaningful to inquire as to whether differences between performances are due to differences in the musicians, or in the violin that is used.

In the same way, while you cannot say whether genes or environment *cause* a particular characteristic displayed by a person, you can examine whether genes or the environment contribute to *differences* in the characteristic across people.

Language is one example of this principle. You certainly need language skills to do well on an IQ test. If you do not understand the instructions, you will not know what you need to do. However, this does not mean that differences in language skills necessarily contribute to *differences* in performance on the IQ test. The instructions may be so simple that everyone taking the test understands what is required of them. Differences in performance on the IQ test may then be due to other factors, such as an inability to understand the abstractions involved.[30]

Understanding Heritability

This principle is also important for understanding estimates of the heritability of different characteristics. Heritability is used to describe the *proportion* of observed differences or variation in a particular trait that is due to genetic factors. In other words, what percentage of differences across people are due to the genes.[31]

Since heritability is a proportion, increasing the contribution of one factor will decrease the relative contribution of the other. If the amount of environmental variation that influences the characteristic increases, this implies that the relative contribution of the genes will go down—along with the heritability estimate. If there is less environmental variation, heritability will go up! So heritability provides an estimate of the *relative* contribution of the genes to differences in the characteristic *based on the current variations in the environment.*

To illustrate this, let us take the example where a characteristic is measured as having 100% heritability. This argues that differences in the characteristic are completely determined by the genes. However, this does not mean that the characteristic can not be affected by the environment, such as if there is some radical new intervention. The 100% heritability only applies when the differences in the environment are equivalent to the differences in the environment that occurred in the group when the heritability estimate was made.

Consider again the example of the violin concerto. What if there are big differences in the expertise of the violinists, and the violins they are using are all quite similar? We would conclude that differences in the performance are largely due to differences in the violinists. However, what if we then introduced large differences in the violins as well? We would then conclude that while the violinists still make an important

51

contribution to the performance, their contribution would be less important than was originally estimated. On the other hand, the estimate of the contribution of the violin itself to the performance would increase. In short, "heritability" is equivalent to an estimate of the relative contribution of the violinist to differences in the performances, based on the range of both violinists and violins that are present when making the estimate.

Implications for Assessing Heritability

This has an important implication. It is often believed that high heritability of a characteristic is undesirable, as it shows that the genes are responsible for most of the differences in the characteristic. However, the above analogy illustrates that high heritability can be a function of the environment being similar across people.

Putting it another way, the best way to decrease the heritability of a trait—or increase the relative contribution of the environment—is for there to be large differences in environmental opportunity across people. These big differences in environmental opportunity will cause big differences in performance, and they will then show that the environment has a great effect on the characteristic. On the other hand, if everyone is given a good environment in which to develop the trait, then the environment will not contribute as much to differences in the characteristic. Heritability will then necessarily increase. So while it is often considered to be undesirable for the heritability of a characteristic to be high, the reality is that this will be the outcome of having a society where every child gets similar environmental opportunities and experiences![32]

THE HERITABILITY OF DIFFERENCES IN IQ

So what then is the heritability of IQ? Are differences in IQ caused by differences in the genes or differences in the environment? This has been a perennial issue that has dogged the study of intelligence. One of the reasons for this seemingly never-ending debate is that psychologists are much more limited than many other scientists in terms of their freedom to carry out the necessary experiments to confirm or refute theories.

What do we mean by this? In science, it is well known that the best way to determine whether a particular factor is responsible for an outcome is to conduct an experiment where the factor is independently manipulated.[33] This typically requires the use of two groups that do not differ at the outset. One group is randomly chosen and administered the factor of interest, while the other group—the control group—is not. The two groups are then evaluated to see whether any differences have resulted. If there is a difference (and it satisfies a statistical test), this indicates that the factor of interest likely caused the difference. The reason this works is because the groups were the same to begin with. Since the factor is the only thing that systematically differs between the groups, it is then likely to be the cause of any subsequent differences between the groups.

As an example of this, consider a chemist who wants to know if a new substance will help a chemical reaction. All she needs to do is perform an experiment whereby the same chemical reaction is carried out twice, once using the new substance, and once without it. By comparing the outcomes, it is possible to determine whether the new substance had an effect on the reaction.

A similar methodology could theoretically be used to determine whether differences in the genes or differences in the environment *cause* differences in intelligence. It would involve taking infants that are the same initially and randomly assigning them to two different environments—impoverished and enriched. If this led to differences between the infants in later life, we could conclude that the environment caused the differences.

However, there is obviously a major problem with conducting such an experiment—it involves deliberately putting some infants in an impoverished environment. Ethical principles rightly prevent us from doing this. However, this lack of ability to do a true experiment, whereby children are randomly assigned to different treatment groups, is also the reason that the nature versus nurture debate has been an issue that has been so difficult for psychology to resolve satisfactorily. Instead, psychology has had to try to determine the role of nature and nurture through more indirect means.

Correlational Studies

One approach to looking at the role of genes and environment in developing intelligence has been to look at correlations between environmental factors and intelligence. For instance, a factor that is frequently believed to be important in influencing a child's intelligence is socioeconomic status. Socioeconomic status is an indicator of a family's economic and social position relative to other families, based on income, education, and occupation.

It is argued that parents with higher socioeconomic status have the resources to provide a better environment for their children. This better environment is then argued to lead to their children having higher intelligence. This claim is supported by the observation that there is a correlation between socioeconomic status and IQ. In other words, children who have higher IQs also tend to come from families that are higher in socioeconomic status.[34]

However, this correlation cannot be used to conclude that the environment *caused* the differences in IQ. An alternative explanation is that the genes are responsible for this correlation. Some parents may have good genes that lead to greater intelligence, and this enables them to attain a higher socioeconomic status. They then pass these genes on to their children, who will also then have greater intelligence—not because of their environment, but because of these genes. Because of this problem, correlational studies are relatively ineffective at determining the contribution of genes and environment to IQ.

Studies of Deprivation

Another approach to studying the role of genes and environment in developing intelligence has been to look at cases where children have been raised in extremely impoverished circumstances. Two such cases were The Wild Boy of Aveyron and Genie.[35]

In both cases, these children were discovered by authorities after living in conditions that lacked basic environmental stimulation for many years. The children did show impaired IQ, suggesting the importance of environmental stimulation for intellectual development.

However, since this was not a true experiment, again there are alternative explanations. For instance, it is possible that these children had deficits in intelligence to begin with, and these deficits may even have contributed to them being kept in such impoverished circumstances.

Further, even if the intellectual impairments were caused by the deprivation, these studies only show that cases of extreme environmental deprivation can have an effect on intellectual functioning. They do not necessarily tell us that the differences in environmental stimulation that children from more typical backgrounds experience would also lead to differences in intelligence. It may be that as long as a child gets a minimal amount of care, they will develop the same intellectual functions irrespective of whatever other differences are present in their environment.

Identical Twin Studies

Psychologists have then sought to use identical twins to resolve the nature versus nurture debate.[36] If a human characteristic is due to the genes, it would be expected to be the same in identical twins—as they have identical genes. On the other hand, if identical twins differ in the characteristic just as much as other children differ, it may be concluded that differences in the environment are solely responsible for differences in the characteristic.

However, using identical twins to resolve the nature versus nurture debate over IQ has also proven difficult. One problem is that while identical twins have identical genes, they are also typically raised in the same family—hence their environments are very similar. Indeed, identical twins often experience environments that are more similar than those experienced by other siblings from the same family. Not only do they typically go to the same school, they are also often in the same classes, and experience events at the same age. Further, since they look the same, assumptions that are made about one twin are likely to be made about the other twin as well. This means that even though identical twins have been found to have IQs that are very similar, it is not clear whether this is due to their identical genes, or the very similar environments they have experienced.

Due to these issues, psychologists have long been interested in identical twins that have been raised apart—a situation that has occurred occasionally when twins have been adopted out to different families at birth. This provides the situation whereby their genes are the same, but now differences in their environments will be more characteristic of those that children from different families experience. These cases have again shown relatively high heritability for IQ.[37]

However, using these cases to conclude that IQ is highly heritable has also been problematic. First, there have actually been very few cases where identical twins have been separated at birth and raised in different families. Another problem has been that, in the cases where identical twins are adopted out to different families, they tend to be adopted out to families that have similar home environments. Therefore, once again, it is difficult to deduce whether similarities in the IQs of identical twins are due to their identical genes or their similar environments.

Adoption Studies

Rather than looking at identical twins, a better test of the relative contribution of genes and environment to IQ has come from looking at adoption studies. These studies examine the effect of the biological and adoptive parents IQ on the IQ of the adopted children.

If differences in IQ were due to the genes, then it would be expected that a child's IQ should be like that of their biological parents—even if they were raised by another family. On the other hand, if differences in IQ are due to the environment, then it would be expected that a child's IQ should be determined more by the environment provided by their adoptive parents than by their biological parents' IQ. This in turn would be related to their adoptive parents' IQ. While not perfect, adoption studies would appear to be the best way to assess the relative roles of the genes and the environment in determining IQ.

Unfortunately, behavioral-genetic studies that look at adoption cases indicate that the genes would certainly appear to play a role. For instance, in response to the controversy created by *The Bell Curve* and its arguments for the high heritability of IQ, the American Psychological Association put together a task force of intelligence researchers from diverse backgrounds. Their task was to provide a definitive statement on what is known and unknown about intelligence. In their report, it was stated that the genes and the environment both contribute about 50% to IQ.[38] This certainly gives authority to the view that both the genes and the environment play an important role in determining differences in performance on IQ tests. Other researchers have estimated the heritability of IQ to be as high as 80%.[39]

CHANGES IN HERITABILITY OVER THE LIFESPAN

Behavioral-genetic studies have gone further than just estimating the role of the genes and the environment in IQ. They have also estimated the heritability of IQ at different ages.[40] This has led to a very surprising finding.

It has been found that the heritability of IQ actually *increases* over childhood. In other words, a person's level of intelligence is more influenced by environmental factors when they are very young. On the other hand, as they approach adulthood, IQ becomes more and more like what would be expected based on their parents' IQ—even if they were adopted out and are no longer living with their biological parents!

This is surprising, as intuitively it would be expected that the effect of the genes should not be increasing over childhood. The genes would seem to be important for the formation of the embryo and its initial development. However, once a child is born, the genes do not change. On the other hand, as they grow older, a child is exposed to more and more environmental experiences. Would this not lead to heritability decreasing rather than increasing?

Between-Family Environment versus Within-Family Environment

In order to better understand this increase in heritability with age, behavioral geneticists have examined different aspects of the environment that contribute to IQ. This has included dividing the environment into two separate components—Between-Family Environment and Within-Family Environment.

Between-Family Environment is used to refer to characteristics of the environment that vary from family to family, and affect children from the same family in the same way. In short, it is called Between-Family Environment because it varies *between families*. Typical examples of Between-Family Environment are socioeconomic status, educational levels of the parents, the number of books in the home, and the quality of the school the children are sent to. The important point is that these characteristics are shared by children in the same family. In other words, all of the children in the family are likely to experience these characteristics similarly. On the other hand, children from other families are likely to differ in these characteristics.

Within-Family Environment is used to refer to characteristics of the environment that differ from one child to the next, even though they are in the same family. In other words, these are differences in the environment that occur *within families*. These environmental factors are typically much more difficult to identify or measure. Some examples would include parents treating one child differently to another, differences between teachers when children are sent to the same school but attend different classes, and the effect of seeing a particular television program at different ages.

Behavioral geneticists have looked at the effect of the Between-Family Environment and the Within-Family Environment on IQ separately. Again, the results have been surprising.

It has been found that the Between-Family Environment does affect IQ at young ages, but the effect diminishes over childhood such that it has little effect on IQ by adulthood. On the other hand, the effect of the Within-Family Environment is found to be moderate and consistent over all of childhood. So the increasing heritability of IQ over childhood is due to the diminishing effect of the Between-Family Environment.

This finding of the diminishing effect of the Between-Family Environment on IQ is surprising because, as was stated earlier, it was originally believed that Between-Family Environment factors such as socioeconomic status would have the largest impact on IQ. Instead, research suggests that these factors do not affect IQ substantially by adulthood!

Again, this can be considered to be a positive outcome. Consider societies of the past. Only the children of wealthy parents would be given access to education and the other opportunities required to maximise potential. This resulted in the Between-Family Environment having a great effect on IQ throughout the lifespan.

In our modern society, the effects of differences in Between-Family Environment are still seen in very young children. However, at later ages, all children are given access to schooling. Even if a child was in an impoverished environment before starting school, schooling would seem to give them the educational experiences required to overcome this impoverished environment. This limits the effect of Between-Family Environment on IQ in later childhood and adulthood.

Of course, this does not mean that Between-Family Environment factors such as parents' wealth do not advantage or disadvantage children in other ways—clearly they do. However, it does at least suggest that IQ is minimally affected in the longer term by differences in the Between-Family Environment.

ENVIRONMENTAL FACTORS THAT INFLUENCE IQ

Given that the environment has been shown to have an effect on IQ, this leads to the question of *what* aspects of the environment are important. The role of environmental experience will be a major focus of this book. However, for now we can note some specific environmental factors that have been identified as either affecting or not affecting IQ.

The time during which a child is gestating in the mother's womb is important. It has been found that prenatal exposure to alcohol, aspirin, and antibiotics can lead to small decreases in IQ.[41] This indicates that it is important for mothers to abstain from these as much as possible while they are pregnant. Major complications associated with birth, including low birth weight, can have serious effects on intellectual development.[42] However, these events are relatively rare, and are typically beyond control in any case. Surprisingly, birth order (whether a child is the oldest in the family, youngest, etc.) and family size are found to have minimal effect on IQ.[43]

Once born, an obvious factor is nutrition. Even within a family, different children can have different dietary preferences. However, research has suggested that nutrition does not have a major effect on IQ unless a child suffers from prolonged malnutrition. Similarly, vitamin and mineral supplements might have an effect. However, the effect is only small, and only in cases where the normal dietary intake is inadequate.[44]

There are also at least a couple of myths about environmental influences on IQ that should be dispelled at this point. One myth that was widely reported was that listening to Mozart could increase intelligence. However, attempts to reproduce this finding have shown that listening to Mozart does not increase IQ. While listening to Mozart can have a small effect on some specific intellectual tasks, this can be attributed to the music making people "happier" and more energetic—especially important when faced with a frustrating intellectual problem. Other manipulations that put people in a better mood can also have a small effect on performance. However, the effect is not permanent. Once a person's mood returns to normal, their performance also falls back to normal.[45]

Another myth has been that teacher's expectations could lead to marked increases in children's IQs. This was based on a study where teachers were told that a randomly-selected group of children were "late bloomers" and due to show a marked spurt within the next year. These children were then shown to have improved intelligence at the end of the year. However, this study was poorly controlled, including the fact that the tests of intelligence were administered by the teachers themselves. It is quite possible that the teachers helped the children to do better on the tests because it was how they believed the children should be doing. Subsequent replications have shown very small effects, if any.[46]

Overall, what is striking is that even though it is known that the environment plays a major role in determining IQ, short-term manipulations of the environment have had only small effects on IQ at best. This suggests that we need a better explanation of what causes IQ if we are to understand how IQ can be manipulated.

CURRENT EXPLANATIONS OF IQ

In order to better understand intelligence, psychologists have focused on the observation we made earlier that performance on one task involving abstractions is related to other tasks involving abstractions. To account for this relation, they have argued that performance on these tasks depends on a common factor. This factor has been labeled the *general factor* of intelligence, or *g*.[47]

It is argued that some people are higher in this *g* factor than others, and some intellectual tasks are argued to depend on *g* to solve them. For instance, it is argued that doing well on Raven's Progressive Matrices depends on a person possessing a high level of *g*. Word Analogies and Number Series also depend on *g*, so a person with a higher level of *g* will do better on these tasks as well. In short, being higher in *g* enables a person to do better across a range of tasks that involve abstractions.

However, this notion of *g* does not provide an explanation of *how* people are able to perform better on tasks that involve understanding abstractions. It merely observes that there is something in common across the tasks. Psychologists have recognized this, and a major goal of intelligence research has been to explain this *g*. We will now look at some of these attempts. It is not necessary for readers to understand these explanations in order to understand the rest of this book, but it will give some background into previous attempts to understand human intelligence.

Brain Size

One early view was that intelligence was related to brain size. It was argued that more intelligent people have bigger brains, much like stronger people have bigger muscles. However, scientific studies have failed to confirm a strong relationship between brain size and intelligence. The relationship that is found is weak, meaning that a person's brain size cannot be taken as a direct indicator of their level of intelligence.[48] Indeed, it is striking that some noted geniuses from the past have had brains that are much smaller than average.[49] For instance, Albert Einstein's brain weighed 1,230 grams, well below the average brain size of between 1,400 and 1,500 grams. Some children have also lost large sections of their brain in early life. However, this loss does not affect their IQ.[50] Again, this suggests that doing better on IQ tests is not simply due to having a larger brain.

Perhaps looking at brain size to identify differences in intelligence is too simple an explanation. We do know that the human brain performs many functions other than abstract thinking, such as sleeping, eating, and controlling movement—similar to the functions performed by animal brains. We also know that the brain is made up of many different parts. These different parts are responsible for these different functions. What if we look for differences in human intelligence only in parts of the human brain that are responsible for abstract thinking?

This has recently been made possible by Magnetic Resonance Imaging (MRI), a technology that produces a picture of the internal structure of a person's brain without surgery. It is similar to X-ray, but produces a much more detailed picture—the resolution is around 1mm. Figure 4 shows a picture of a person's brain using MRI.

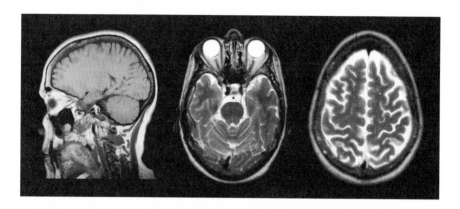

Figure 4. Magnetic Resonance Imaging (MRI) scans of the brain showing the level of detail that is possible. Note that internal structures of the brain are also revealed.

This technology has revealed that there are great differences across people, not only in brain size, but also in the size and shape of different regions and structures throughout the brain. However, what is striking is that these differences do not seem to have a major effect on behavior. Studies comparing these differences and IQ or other measures of intellectual function have shown only small and inconsistent correlations.[51] This suggests that it is not possible to tell what causes differences in IQ or the ability to understand abstractions by looking at the overall size of brain parts. Instead, the difference is likely due to what goes on in these brain regions.

Digital Computer Metaphor

Because the size of brain structures does not seem to be related to IQ, psychologists have sought to understand human intelligence by examining how the brain actually processes or computes information.

One early idea was to draw an analogy between the human brain and the digital computer. This is because, superficially, brains and digital computers appear to be similar. They both receive input, such as letters on a page or numbers typed in, and they both produce output, such as an answer to an abstraction problem or the sum of a column of numbers. Since the input and the output are not the same, there is some mechanism that processes or transforms the information. Perhaps, then, digital computers can tell us what causes differences in human intelligence?

However, many readers will already be aware of a problem with this. In Chapter One, we reviewed how digital computers are quite different to humans. Tasks that humans find easy, such as perceiving an apple, are tasks that even the most advanced digital computers find challenging. On the other hand, even a home computer can calculate in seconds the total of a large spreadsheet that it would take a human years to do.

This presents a problem for the digital computer metaphor. The sorts of tasks that digital computers find so difficult to do, such as perceiving abstractions, are exactly the types of tasks that are central to perform-ing well on IQ tests. This suggests that the digital computer and how it processes information will be a poor model for understanding how the human brain is able to understand abstractions. Perhaps not surpris-ingly, psychologists who have used the digital computer metaphor have failed to explain differences in human intelligence.

Speed of Information Processing

Another idea that may be related to the digital computer metaphor is the notion that speed of processing may explain differences in intelli-gence. Computers have been getting faster over time. This has increased the functions that they are able to perform. Originally, it was not possible to play a video on the computer or even view a document in the way it would look when printed out, due to the number of calculations required. However, as computers have become faster, these functions are now commonplace. Perhaps speed is the underlying cause of differences in IQ as well? In other words, a brain that can process information faster will be more intelligent.[52]

However, we can immediately note that a difference in intelligence is not just a difference in speed. It is not the case that someone with a low IQ has the same ability to solve problems as a high IQ-person—the only difference being that it takes them longer. Tests of abstraction such as Raven's Progressive Matrices are often given without a time limit. If someone has difficulty understanding the abstractions involved, they cannot provide the correct solution—no matter how much time they are given.

It is also found that there are only modest correlations between the time it takes to do simple tasks and intelligence.[53] Direct measures of the speed at which signals are transmitted in the nervous system have also failed to show a relationship with intelligence.[54] This suggests that the relationship between speed of information processing and intelligence is complex.

However, even more problematic is that speed of information processing does not *explain* intelligence. Recall that intelligence tests consist of perceiving or understanding abstractions. How would faster speed of information processing actually lead to *better* understanding? With faster speed of information processing, an answer will be arrived at sooner, but this does not mean that it will be more correct. This suggests that faster speed of information processing is not a sufficient explanation in itself for the superior ability to perceive or understand abstractions.

Working Memory Capacity

Another explanation put forward by psychologists has centered on working memory capacity.[55] Working memory capacity is argued to be a measure of the capacity to "store and process" information. More intelligent people are said to have greater working memory capacity. This greater capacity, it is claimed, leads to them being more able to solve intelligence problems.

However, again, this is not providing an explanation of differences in intelligence. We know that there are differences in the ability to "store and process" information. The goal is to understand what causes these differences. Labeling these differences as "working memory capacity" is not explaining these differences. It is only giving them another name.

The working memory capacity explanation has further difficulties. It was originally based on observing a correlation in performance between working memory capacity tasks and intelligence tasks. However, an examination of the working memory capacity tasks indicates that they are very similar to the intelligence tasks. If the tasks involve the same underlying operations, then finding that they are related is not surprising.

Therefore, researchers have tried to define working memory capacity tasks using criteria that are independent to intelligence tests. However, it turns out that tasks fitting these criteria do not always correlate with intelligence tasks.[56] To avoid this problem, only working memory capacity tasks that meet the criteria *and correlate with intelligence* are defined as true working memory capacity tasks.[57] However, if you need to rely on the correlation with intelligence to define a working memory capacity task, it means that you are not explaining intelligence using an explanation that is independent to intelligence itself.

Another problem with working memory capacity is similar to that encountered with speed of information processing, namely that it does not actually *explain* the ability to understand abstractions. The challenge in perceiving abstractions is to filter out information that is unique to a concrete instance, and only be aware of information that is consistent across concrete instances. Having greater working memory capacity should result in more information being represented in the mind, including information that is unique to concrete instances. Therefore, people with greater working memory capacity should have greater difficulty perceiving abstractions—so they should actually show lower intelligence. The working memory capacity explanation also does not explain how the right information is filtered out to enable the recognition of different abstractions. This mechanism is left unspecified.[58]

Some recent studies have found that experience on working memory capacity tasks can lead to a small increase in IQ.[59] However, it is not uncommon for other experimental manipulations to also lead to a small increase in IQ. These increases often come about because other factors such as motivation and confidence also play a role in performing well on IQ tests. Manipulations can affect these other factors. However, these manipulations are only temporary, and do not represent major changes in IQ test performance. Only when training on working memory capacity tasks is shown to have a major effect on IQ could it be claimed that working memory capacity is the underlying cause of differences in IQ. Attempts to show this so far have been unsuccessful.[60]

A SATISFACTORY EXPLANATION OF IQ IS STILL NEEDED

We can see that none of the current theories put forward by psychologists really provide an explanation of IQ and human intelligence. This is not controversial. Experts in the field openly acknowledge that a satisfactory explanation of intelligence is yet to be given.[61]

What is missing from these theories is an explanation of abstraction. As was discussed in Chapter One, it is readily acknowledged that abstraction is central to human intelligence—so any theory of intelligence that fails to account for the ability to perceive or understand abstractions is missing an essential component of intelligence. However, brain science has also made major advances recently. It turns out that this research gives us the information we need to understand abstraction and human intelligence.

CHAPTER FOUR

WHAT BRAIN SCIENCE TELLS US ABOUT UNDERSTANDING

Huge strides have been made in our understanding of the brain over the last few decades. However, as previously mentioned, it is important to realize that the brain does much more than just "thinking." It is responsible for many other functions that we often take for granted.

For instance, when you decide to walk across the room, you do not need to think about moving each leg forward and bending your ankle to make contact with the ground. Similarly, you know when you feel hungry or tired, and will eat or sleep when you need to. Even breathing is something that needs to be controlled so that your blood has the appropriate level of oxygen in it. All of these functions are controlled by the brain, and other animals such as cats and mice also have brains that allow them to perform these functions.

At the same time, humans are capable of more adaptable and flexible behaviors than any other animal, particularly due to our use of abstractions. So we first need to identify what parts or regions of the brain are likely to be important for the human capacity to "think" and understand abstractions.

A MAP OF THE BRAIN

Much of the original research into the function of different brain regions was based on the effects of brain damage. More recently, technologies such as functional Magnetic Resonance Imaging (fMRI) have allowed researchers to observe activity in a person's brain while they are awake, without the need for surgery. fMRI is like the MRI that we talked about in the previous chapter. However, rather than just providing an image of the brain, it also measures changes in blood flow. It is argued that if blood flow to a brain region increases while a person is doing a task, then that region plays a role in performing the task.

Studies of brain function have revealed that the cerebral cortex is the brain region where "thinking" takes place.[62] Figure 5 shows the cerebral cortex. It is the wrinkles that surround much of the brain. The cerebral cortex is actually a sheet. However, if it was laid out flat, it would be much too large to fit inside the skull. To enable it to fit, the sheet is crumpled up, in much the same way that you can fit a large piece of paper into a cup by crumpling it up. The wrinkles that we see are due to this crumpling.

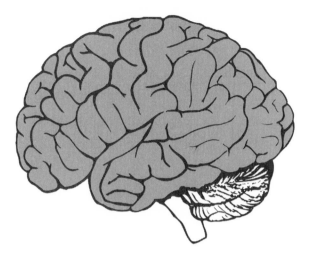

Figure 5. An illustration of the brain, highlighting the cerebral cortex (shaded region). The cerebral cortex surrounds many of the other parts of the brain.

However, it is not only humans that have a cerebral cortex. Other animals such as chimpanzees, dogs, and mice all have a cerebral cortex as well. The big difference is that while the cerebral cortex exists in these other animals' brains, it is smaller. And when we say smaller, we do not just mean in terms of total volume. If you enlarged other animals' brains so that they were the same size as the human brain, you would find that the cerebral cortex was still relatively smaller in other animals. So, when we compare the human brain with the brains of other animals, we not only see that the whole brain is larger, but also that most of the difference in size is due to the increased size of the cerebral cortex.[63]

This increase in size of the cerebral cortex parallels the increase in flexibility of humans. We are very flexible in terms of producing differing behaviors based on different situations. We do this because we *understand* that a behavior that works in one situation may not necessarily work in another situation. Animals tend to be more stereotyped in their behavior—meaning that they will produce the same behavior in many different situations without understanding that sometimes it will work, but other times it will not. Anyone who has had a dog barking outside, wanting you to throw their ball, even though it is raining and it is 6 a.m., or who has observed a dog repeatedly trying to run between two trees with a stick, even though the stick is too long to fit through the gap, can testify to this.

Understanding in the Brain

Studies of the cerebral cortex have made another striking observation. When we think, it seems as though our thoughts take place in a single location—whether we are thinking of a square, thinking of the sound a cat makes, or imagining what it feels like to pick up an apple. However, it has been found that different regions of the cerebral cortex are activated for each of these thoughts.

For instance, when we think of a square, a region of the cerebral cortex near the back of the head—where input from our eyes enter—is activated. When we think of the sound a cat makes, another region of the cerebral cortex that is attached to input from the ears is activated. Another region again is activated when we think about touching an object.[64]

Brain damage can also result in disordered thinking in only very specific categories.[65] Someone with one form of brain damage may function normally, except that they cannot recognize tools or what they are used for. Damage to another region may only affect someone's ability to recognize or understand living things. Damage to one side of the brain can result in someone only being "aware" of objects on one side of their vision. They may only shave the right side of their face, and will believe that they have finished eating once they have consumed all of the food on one side of their plate.[66]

What this tells us is that different parts of the cerebral cortex are responsible for us thinking about different kinds of information. There is no central region that is responsible for "understanding" from all different domains, even though it may seem like this when we experience understanding ourselves. Understanding is distributed throughout the cortex.[67]

Myths about the Brain

When talking about brain regions, we can also dispel a couple of myths. One is the belief that there is a sharp distinction between the left and right hemispheres of the cerebral cortex in the information they process. The "left brain" is argued to be important for logical and rational thought. The "right brain" is argued to be more responsible for creativity. It is also argued that people may be either "left-brained" or "right-brained." However, while it is found that different sides of the brain can process different kinds of information, it is a crude generalization to define their differences in any clear-cut way. It is even more misleading to say that people are either "left-brained" or "right-brained." All people use both sides of their brain. Psychological research has not provided strong support for the left-brain versus right-brain generalization, or the idea that you can selectively train one hemisphere or the other.[68]

Another myth that is commonly heard is that we only use 10% of our brains. Not only is there no evidence to support this, brain scientists do not even know where this idea came from![69] In fact, the converse is actually true. Irrespective of differences in brain size and structure across people, research has found that all parts of the brain will perform at least some function.

For instance, people who are born blind do not have visual input entering the back of their brain like normal-sighted people. However, the back region of their brain does not remain inactive. It has been found that this area is then used for the processing of other sensory information, such as sounds and touch.[70] Similarly, if a child is born with major damage to one hemisphere, it has been found that the intact hemisphere will take over and perform the functions of both hemispheres.[71] The right hemisphere can even perform the language functions that are typically located in the left hemisphere.

This points to an amazing ability of the brain to reorganize and use the same brain region for different tasks. This flexibility is what enables humans to behave successfully even if their development takes very different paths, such as cases of brain damage. The success of this reorganization would also suggest that different cortical regions use a common mechanism to process information. This mechanism will be a major focus of this book.

THE MAIN CELLS IN THE BRAIN—NEURONS

If we are to understand intelligence in the brain, we need to go beyond the question of which brain regions are responsible for intelligence. We need to look at how these regions *work*. This includes looking at the cells that make up these regions, understanding how they interact to lead, ultimately, to intelligent behavior.

It is found that the brain is composed of cells called neurons. Each neuron has a number of branches that emerge from the cell body, and these branches form connections with other neurons. These connections allow neurons to communicate with each other. Some of these branches are for receiving inputs from other neurons and are called dendrites. Other branches are for sending information. These are called axons. Figure 6 is a simplified illustration of a neuron in the cerebral cortex. Neurons can vary in size and shape, but they always have branches responsible for either receiving or sending information.

Individual neurons will be connected to individual receptors in the sense organs, such as those providing visual and auditory information. These neurons will then carry information specific to that receptor, such as the presence of light at a particular point in the visual field or a sound of a particular pitch and amplitude. Other neurons will then connect to these neurons and project the information further into the brain. Eventually, yet more neurons will receive inputs from

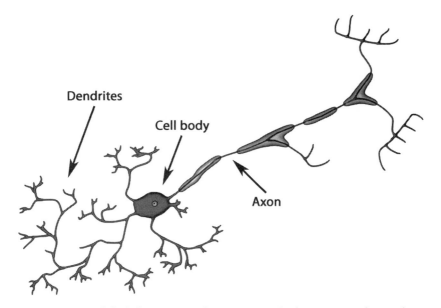

Figure 6. A simplified illustration of a neuron in the brain. Note that real neurons have many more connections than are shown here, and the axons can project from one region of the brain to another.

these other neurons, transmit their signals to the muscles, and lead to movement.

The same types of neurons can be found in many different animals. In fact, exactly the same neurons found in the human brain are also found in the brains of other mammals including chimpanzees, cats, and mice. This tells us that human intelligence is not due to any special type of neuron that other animals do not possess.[72]

The Complexity of the Brain

What Figure 6 does not show is the complexity of the human brain. It is estimated that each neuron has, on average, 50,000 connections with other neurons. However, despite each neuron having all of these connections, neurons are also incredibly small. It is estimated that there are around 100,000 neurons in a cubic millimeter of the cerebral cortex. This means that there are literally billions of neurons and trillions of connections in the total brain![73]

This complexity highlights the limitations of current technologies that are used to study the brain such as fMRI. The resolution of fMRI is about one cubic millimeter, so it is summarizing the activity—or rather blood flow—to a block of 100,000 neurons. This is an incredibly crude measure of what is occurring in the brain. It falls a long way short of telling us what is occurring in the brain at the level of an individual neuron.

This small size means that neurons are typically studied with microscopes, and sometimes even electron microscopes. These tools require cutting the brain into thin slices, which precludes an examination of a person's neural connections while they are still alive. Even if the brains of people who have died are studied, the complexity of the brain makes it impossible to work out how all of the neurons are connected. Not only are the number of neurons and connections astronomical, but the mere act of cutting the neural tissue into slices results in much of the information about the neural connections being scrambled and lost.

Despite this, microscopic investigation of the neurons has provided important information about the neural connections in the brain. These studies have revealed that, despite the sheer number of neural connections, the connections are not uniform or symmetric. Rather, the pattern of connections shown by one neuron is unlikely to be similar to the patterns of connections shown by other neurons. Also, adjacent neurons are unlikely to be connected to each other. Neurons will be very precise in terms of which neurons they *do* and *do not* connect to. Perhaps not surprisingly, this complexity of the connections is most evident in the cerebral cortex, the region that is responsible for human intelligence.[74]

How Neurons Work

When imagining the massive network of neural connections in the brain, it is tempting to think of them as being like a train network. With a train network, a line will often branch off into separate lines going to different destinations. When a train reaches a branching point, a switch can be thrown that will send the train down one line or the other. In this way, a train can go from any location in the rail network to any other location.

If this analogy was true for the brain, it would mean that a signal from one neuron could lead to the activation of any other neuron in the network through the massive number of connections between the neurons. However, for the brain to work in the same way as a train network, neurons would need to be able to act like the points or switches in a train network.

Consider character recognition. Being presented with a letter "T" on the page should lead to a signal being sent to whatever represents the letter "T" in the brain. On the other hand, being presented with the letter "S" should send a signal to somewhere else in the brain that represents "S". Indeed, this is how our brains seem to intuitively work. It seems as though when we see the letter "T," stimulation from the receptors in our eyes lead to a representation of "T" in our brain. When we see the letter "S," stimulation from the same receptors gets switched over so that activation in our brain then represents an "S."

Indeed, up until fifty years ago, it was also believed in neuroscience that this was how neurons worked—that they were switches that allowed signals to be directed around the brain based on the meaning of the signals.

However, in the past few decades, research has enabled a comprehensive understanding of neurons to be developed.[75] This has included artificially stimulating neurons to learn how they respond, and investigating the mechanisms that underlie their operation. This research has shown that neurons are *not* switches. They cannot redirect inputs, or turn inputs on and off from one moment to the next as we are presented with different experiences. Rather than being switches, neurons are simple gating mechanisms. If they receive input that is strong enough from other neurons, they will send a signal. This signal will then be carried to all the branches of the neuron's axon. This transmission process is based on basic chemical processes such as diffusion that have no knowledge of what the signal represents. It is like the propagation of the waves that are produced when a rock hits the surface of a pool of water—the waves progress outwards from the source, obeying basic laws of physics. There is no way that the brain can switch the signal so that it moves along one connection and not another.

80

Avoiding a Homunculus

Perhaps astute readers will not be surprised to learn that neurons are not in fact switches. After all, the problem with arguing that neurons behave as switches becomes—who is controlling the switches? If the neurons were switches, it would imply that there is a controller controlling the switches, deciding what information is important and where in the brain it should go—in the same way a train controller determines where the trains will go in a rail network.

This, then, begs the question—how does this controller know what to do? The requirements for intelligent decision making have not been explained, but simply transferred to some mythical entity that knows what to do. Does this controller then have another controller that tells it what to do? How does this other controller know what to do?

This is known as the *homunculus problem* in psychology—the situation where an "explanation" of behavior does not actually explain the behavior, but simply relies on some unknown mechanism for the explanation. It is called the homunculus problem because it is like saying that there is a little human (or homunculus) in the brain that is responsible for humans behaving intelligently. For instance, the little human in the brain knows what the different signals mean, and switches the neurons to lead to intelligent behavior. However, there is no explanation of how this little human knows what switches to use, or how it is able to be intelligent. This is not a satisfactory explanation.

THE IMPORTANCE OF THE CONNECTIONS

So if the neurons do not act as switches, how is the brain able to behave intelligently? How are signals able to be filtered, such that some are transmitted and others are not, based on their importance?

Think back to the challenge of perceiving abstractions that we discussed in Chapter One. Our eye has thousands of receptors that provide information about what we are looking at. However, much of this information is irrelevant. If we are reading a book, the exact type of font used, its size, the color of the writing and paper, the amount of lighting present, and what is on the desk next to the book, are all irrelevant to understanding what the text is saying.

If the brain consisted of all neurons being connected to all other neurons, then all of this information would get transmitted up to and through the brain. We would have an exact concrete picture of what we are seeing. However, we would not be able to associate this scene with other scenes we experienced when we learned to read. While there would be some similarities—such as the shapes of the letters—this would be outweighed by all of the differences between the situations. Differences in the exact font, its size, the color of the writing and paper, the amount of lighting, and new objects on our desk would mean that the situations would seem to be drastically different.

If this was the case, you would be able to read words written on a blackboard at your old primary school since this is where you learned to read. However, this information would not generalize to reading a book on your desk at home, or a street sign. Too much information would be different.

Indeed, infants have this very problem. Infants can be trained to kick to activate a mobile in their crib—an activity that gives them enjoyment.[76] If they are then given the mobile the next day, they will again kick to activate it. They know that their kicking will produce an event that they like. However, what if some aspect of their surrounding environment unrelated to the mobile is changed, such as their crib liner? Once this change is made, they will no longer kick to activate the mobile. Even though the mobile is the same in both situations, they do not recognize the similarity—because enough of the environment has changed.

This again illustrates that an ability that we take for granted as adults—recognizing objects independent of their context—is a challenging task that we are not born with, but develops slowly over childhood.

So, how can the brain see similarity between situations? In other words, how can the brain ignore or filter out information that is irrelevant to a commonality across situations, allowing it to generalize what it knows from one situation to another? We have already learned that neurons are not switches, so irrelevant information cannot be simply switched off.

The answer that has been established over the past few decades by many brain researchers, and through various different research techniques, is actually quite simple—by physically *changing* the connections between the neurons. By changing the connections, only those neurons that should be communicating with each other are able to do so. Rather than the brain behaving like a train network able to send trains anywhere, it only lays down train tracks based on the specific locations where the trains need to go.

This explains why the brain is seen to have such complex and idiosyncratic connections. These connections determine the path of signals in the brain. In short, it is these connections, or the wiring diagram of the brain, in which intelligence is held. They make intelligent behavior possible. A complex wiring diagram enables the brain to send signals to the appropriate locations, as opposed to a simple or uniform connection pattern that would not send signals to different parts of the brain based on their significance or relevance.

Changes in the Connections over the Lifespan

The next question we can ask is—how do the neural connections change over the lifespan? Here, the findings are surprising. For instance, it has been found that the cerebral cortex has more neurons at birth than at any time thereafter. Indeed, the number of neurons in the brain falls dramatically over childhood.[77] While there is evidence that new neurons are formed in the adult brain, this is restricted to brain regions responsible for memory that we will learn about later.[78] New neurons in adulthood are not found in the regions of the cerebral cortex where abstraction takes place.

This decrease in neurons over childhood is surprising, as you would initially expect that having more neurons would be better. After all, it is neurons that allow the brain to process information. However, as we have already learned, infants are not more intelligent than adults. In fact, the ability to understand abstractions gradually improves over childhood to adulthood. So this suggests that more neurons are not necessarily better, and can even hurt when it comes to perceiving abstractions.

However, what about the neural connections themselves? Again, the findings are surprising. It has been observed that the infant cerebral cortex has many more neurons, but relatively few connections. Over childhood, the number of connections will grow massively at first. This enormous growth results in a situation where the child's brain can actually have many *more* connections than it will have in adulthood. Despite this greater number of connections, the child is still worse than an adult at understanding abstractions. This indicates that just having lots of neural connections also does not result in greater intelligence.

This observation has also been confirmed using computer simulations of neural networks.[79] In these computer simulations, nodes with characteristics similar to neurons are created. Connections between them are also simulated. The connections can then be tuned such that the network makes some form of response that we consider meaningful—such as recognizing letters that are printed on a page. If connections are then simply added to the network, the performance of the network will go down.

The reason for this was explained in the previous section. The tuned network is able to produce its meaningful behavior because only particular neurons are connected to other particular neurons. In this way, activity is able to be meaningfully channeled around the network. If more connections are added, this means that information is transmitted not just between the neurons that should be connected to produce the appropriate response, but also to other neurons that carry irrelevant information. Hence, the network will eventually just produce the same response, irrespective of what letter it is presented with.

The Pruning Process

So what happens after the child's brain has grown all of these neural connections? It then goes through a process that has been described by brain scientists as *pruning*.[80] Essentially, the number of connections in the child's brain is reduced, while those connections that are retained are strengthened. So, rather than having many connections in a uniform pattern, as the child becomes older the connections reduce in number, and also become more and more idiosyncratic or specific in the neurons to which they connect.

The timing of this pruning process also varies from one region of the cerebral cortex to another. Regions that are associated with processing early sensory information, such as visual and auditory input, show this process of a progressive increase and then decrease in the neural connections such that adult levels of neural connections are reached by age five.

On the other hand, this process takes longer in other regions. In some regions, particularly the regions that seem to be responsible for the highest-level abstract thought, it is not until late adolescence that the regions reach adult levels of neural connections.[81]

We can see, then, that the time frame of this pruning process corresponds to the time frame over which the ability to understand abstractions develops. Young children are poor at understanding abstractions at a time when the brain regions that process abstractions show a different pattern of neural connections than what is possessed in adulthood. As these areas progressively reduce their neural connections through pruning during childhood and adolescence, the ability to understand abstractions increases. Once the neural connections have finished pruning at around sixteen years of age, the capacity to understand abstractions is at a maximum.

IS THE CHANGE IN CONNECTIONS DUE TO GENES OR ENVIRONMENT?

Given that there seems to be a relationship between the development of the neural connections and the development of the ability to understand abstractions, a critical question then is—what causes the development of the neural connections? Is it due to the genes or the environment?

Purely on logical grounds, it can be argued that it is due to the environment rather than the genes. After all, abstractions are general principles of the *environment*, so it stands to reason that it is experience with the environment that leads to the development of the neural connections that allow abstractions to be perceived or identified.

Further, if all of the information required to develop the neural connections was present in the genes, this begs the question of why evolution did not lead to infants being born with high intelligence. Why does the ability to understand abstractions take so long to develop?

In fact, it is known that one of the major differences between humans and other animals is that human infants are born much more helpless than other animals. Other animals can navigate their environment and sense predators immediately after being born. Because human infants develop slower, they are much more at risk of harm. If the information required for understanding abstractions was contained within the genes, then it would make sense for it to be expressed early on. It would be expected that even young children would have an ability to understand or perceive abstractions comparable to that of adults—even if their actual concrete knowledge or expertise about the world was much less.

However, in addition to logical arguments, empirical evidence also argues strongly against the notion that genes determine the gradual development of the neural connections over childhood.

For instance, it has been known for a long time that human DNA does not possess an astronomical number of genes. The human genome project has mapped the entire human DNA and revealed that there are only around 25,000 genes.[82] These 25,000 genes are not only responsible for brain development, but for the development of the rest of the body as well!

Consider this number relative to the number of neural connections that we discussed earlier. It is known that the brain contains *billions* of neurons and *trillions* of connections. It was also observed that these connections do not form simple or uniform patterns, but are very idiosyncratic, suggesting that it would take a huge amount of information to summarize their connection patterns. Hence, there is no way that the genes could be coding the individual neural connections in the brain.

The view that the genes play a crucial role in specifying individual neural connections encounters further problems when changes from species to species are taken into account. It is found that there is an astronomical increase in the number of connections as we move from chimpanzees to humans. On the other hand, chimpanzees have 98.8% of their DNA in common with humans.[83] This implies that there are as little as 500 genes that differentiate us from chimpanzees! Even if all of these genes were devoted to intelligence, there is no way that 500 genes could code all of the differences in connections that would lead to the markedly superior intelligence of humans. What is striking, in contrast, is that human intelligence has arisen with so little additional genetic material.

Brain science has also not found any evidence of mechanisms that could allow specific genes or DNA segments to code for specific neural connections in the cerebral cortex. How would the genes be able to distinguish between all of the neurons throughout the brain when there are literally billions of similar neurons? How would the genes know the appropriate neurons to form connections to? Brain science has shown that the genes are responsible for forming general connection patterns early in development.[84] However, the later sculpting of the neural connections through the pruning process involves too much specificity to be due to the genes.

We may also consider identical twins, who have the same genes or DNA. Do their brains have identical connections? Studies comparing the brains of even relatively simple animals with identical genes have found that they do not have identical neural connections.[85] In human identical twins, even major brain structures can be different sizes and shapes, indicating that the underlying neural tissue, including its connections, is substantially different.[86]

All of these observations suggest that the genes do not specify the changes in the neural connections that occur over childhood.

Environmental Influence

If the genes are not responsible, what about the environment? There is now extensive evidence that the development of the neural connections over childhood is due to environmental experience. Researchers have described the ability of the brain to change in response to the environment as "plasticity."[87] The term "plasticity" reflects the observation that the neural connections seem to be like Plasticine or Play-Doh. They can be molded to different shapes, rather than being fixed or rigid.

This capacity to physically change the neural connections is very different to that of machines we typically build. When we manufacture machines, the design or structure of the machine is determined prior to production. It will not change once the machine has been produced. For instance, a car that is required to pull heavy loads will not develop a more powerful engine over time. The structure of the engine will stay the same, irrespective of the environmental demands placed on it. Even digital computers have their circuits or connections laid down in silicon. The silicon crystal is rigid, with the possible paths that electrons can take being the same from the date of manufacture until the computer is replaced.

However, this rigidity, or lack of change, is not a hallmark of biology. If someone lifts weights, their muscles become bigger and stronger. If someone contracts a disease, the body develops an immune response so it is more resistant to the disease in the future. Biology often adapts or changes itself over time based on the nature of the environment it is experiencing. This is a more flexible solution. It enables biological organisms to be suited to different requirements without these adaptations needing to be built into the genes and evolved over hundreds or thousands of generations.

Plasticity in the Cerebral Cortex

David Hubel and Torsten Wiesel were the first to systematically study plasticity in the cerebral cortex. For this research, they received the 1981 Nobel Prize in Physiology or Medicine.[88] They found that altering the visual experience of a kitten during infancy would change the neural connections in the visual region of the cerebral cortex. If one eye was shut at birth, then neural connections from that eye would be lost. This indicated that visual stimulation, which would cause the receptors in the eye to become activated, was necessary to develop the connections of the neurons attached to these receptors.

More recent research has shown that characteristics of visual stimulation affect the nature of the connections that are formed in the visual cortex. This, in turn, determines what neurons in the visual cortex represent. For instance, vertical and horizontal lines represent points of light appearing together in different orientations. If a kitten is exposed to only vertical lines of light during infancy, it will develop connections to represent only vertical lines. It will then be unable to perceive horizontal lines in later life.[89] If a kitten is exposed to only spots of light from

90

birth, it will be more sensitive in later life to spots of light than to lines of any orientation.[90]

In the last few decades, much research has shown that the cerebral cortex needs environmental experience to develop. It uses environmental experience to tell it which neurons convey useful information and should have connections developed.[91]

Critical or Sensitive Periods

Another striking finding of this research is that this process only occurs during so-called "critical" or "sensitive" periods.[92] This means that neurons can change their connections in response to environmental stimulation, but this process only occurs during a particular *age range* or "window" of development. Stimulation during this period results in the connections changing, but the same stimulation at other times does not have the same effect.

Consider again the example of visual stimulation received by kittens. If you *prevent* a kitten from seeing horizontal lines in infancy, it will be unable to perceive horizontal lines in later life. No matter how much you present the adult cat with horizontal lines, it will still be unable to perceive them.

On the other hand, if you *do* present a kitten with horizontal lines in infancy, it will be able to perceive horizontal lines in later life. It will have no difficulty perceiving them even if you provide them with a visual environment in adulthood that does not include horizontal lines for an extended period of time. No matter how long they are exposed to the environment without horizontal lines in adulthood, they will never lose the ability to perceive horizontal lines when tested!

A similar sensitive period for vision is also found in humans. With children, the sensitive period for the development of vision is from birth up until around five years of age.[93] This corresponds with observations that the visual cortex in children finishes its pruning process at five years of age.

This sensitive period means that a child's vision is likely to be permanently impaired if one of their eyes is covered for a prolonged period before age five. For example, if their eye is bandaged due to some form of injury. It does not matter how much normal visual input the child receives once the eye is uncovered—the lack of stimulation during the sensitive period profoundly influences neural development.

While this may come across as pessimistic, it is simply acknowledging the reality that biology does influence our development. This recognition has meant that cases of visual impairment due to covering the eye during early childhood have been substantially reduced. Doctors now know that covering the eye during this time can lead to permanent impairment. Therefore, they try to ensure that the eye receives appropriate stimulation during the sensitive period.

It has also been found that covering the eye for a lengthy period after five years of age has no permanent effect on vision. This indicates that once the neural connections have finished their pruning process, they retain this configuration indefinitely—whether environmental stimulation is present or not.

Other evidence confirming the sensitive period for the development of vision is provided by cases of people who have had cataracts on their eyes since birth. This prevents normal visual input from entering their eyes. In some cases, these cataracts have been surgically removed in adulthood. However, the removal of the cataracts has not enabled these individuals to see normally. It has been found that they never develop visual functions that people who have received normal visual input in childhood take for granted. This includes the ability to quickly identify shapes and assess distance.[94]

So, findings such as these indicate that environmental stimulation during childhood is essential if the neural connections are to develop properly.

HOW THE CONNECTIONS ARE DETERMINED

We have already learned how the pruning of the neural connections occurs over the time during which the ability to understand abstractions increases. This suggests that the pruning process might be responsible for the increasing ability to understand abstractions. However, we now know much more about the mechanism by which the neural connections change in response to experience during this time.[95]

It is found that each neural connection will have a "growth cone" on its tip. This growth cone will guide the growth of the connection, determining which neuron the connection will attach to. How does the growth cone know which neuron to seek out? Researchers have found the growth cone will be attracted to chemicals in the brain known as "growth factors." Other neurons release these growth factors. The growth cone will take up this growth factor, and then grow towards its source. This enables the connection to find a neuron to attach to.

However, this is not the whole story. The neurons only release a limited amount of growth factor—not enough for all of the nearby connections. This means that the connections will compete with each other for the limited amount of growth factor that is available. Those that receive the growth factor will grow and form a connection with the neuron that is releasing the growth factor, while those that do not receive the growth factor will withdraw. If they do not find growth factor from any other neurons, they will eventually die. This leads to the pruning process that is observed in the developing cerebral cortex. There is not enough growth factor for all of the neurons and connections, so the excess neurons and connections are "pruned" or lost.[96]

So, what determines whether growth factor will be released, as well as whether a growth cone will grow towards it? It is based on *activity* of the neurons. Only an *active* neuron will release growth factor. Other neurons that are *active at the same time* will then grow towards and make connections with the neuron that has released the growth factor.

This tells us why activity or experience plays such a crucial role in developing the neural connections. When an eye is shut during childhood, the neurons attached to the eye are not active—so they do not attempt to make connections with other neurons. Similarly, in the case of vertical lines, receptors that are in a vertical line are active together. If all of these are active together, they will form connections on the same neuron. The neuron they connect to will then "represent" the vertical line.

This neural process of pruning the neural connections through growth processes is now well understood biologically. Computer simulations of this process have also resulted in connection patterns that are similar to what is observed in the human brain.[97,98]

Developing Abstractions

So, what does this pruning process have to do with the increasing ability to understand abstractions that occurs over childhood?

It turns out that this learning process has exactly the right characteristics to lead to abstractions. You will recall what we observed in Chapter One. Abstractions are where the information specific to concrete instances is lost, and information that is in common across concrete instances is retained. This is what the neural connections are doing as they prune over childhood!

Information that is unique to a particular concrete instance is not frequently experienced—so connections representing this information will be lost. On the other hand, information that is consistent across concrete instances is frequently experienced—so connections that represent this information will be retained and strengthened. In this way, by experiencing many different concrete instances over childhood, the brain gradually changes its connections to extract the commonality across the situations and ignore information that varies from one concrete instance to the next. This leads to abstract representations.

Once this is done, the changes in the connections allow adults to perceive abstractions automatically and seemingly effortlessly. Information that is unique to the concrete instance is automatically filtered out because these connections have been lost, and only information that occurs across situations is retained. The similarity between two situations with a common abstraction is then seen, and knowledge from one situation can be used in another situation.[99]

As children become older, they then have the ability to understand more and more abstractions as their neural connections have been pruned to show the commonality across more and more events. The ability to understand abstractions is at a maximum in young adulthood as this is when the pruning process has been operational for the longest time—meaning that a young adult has had the benefit of the pruning process occurring throughout their entire childhood. The ability to understand abstractions then likely starts to decline in later adulthood due to other aging processes that affect the elderly brain.[100]

Eliminating the Homunculus

Notice that this process also eliminates the homunculus problem, which referred to the problem of how the brain is able to produce intelligent responses without needing a little intelligent person inside saying what information is relevant and irrelevant. In other words, how does the brain know which elements represent a commonality across situations and should be attended to, and which elements are unique to a concrete instance and should be ignored?

Pruning the connections over childhood means that a homunculus is not required to switch off irrelevant elements when an abstraction is encountered in adulthood. Over childhood, many concrete instances of an abstraction are encountered. This allows the brain to learn about the existence of the abstraction *through exposure alone.* The many concrete instances tell the brain which connections to eliminate. The elimination of those connections enables the abstraction to be seen subsequently in different contexts or concrete instances.

Consider again the simple example of recognizing the letter "T." The letter "T" is an abstraction that consists of two lines intersecting at the top. Recognizing the letter "T" involves being sensitive to this information and ignoring other information such as the exact font type, size, and color. Once children have learned to read, they can read text in many different contexts. This includes contexts where a novel font is used, or a new color. They are able to do this because their brain has learned to ignore this information when reading. It is irrelevant to the information that indicates the presence of the letter, and which is in common across all situations that involve the letter. As long as the lines are present in the right way, their brain will detect this information and the letter "T" will be perceived.

So, we can see that recognizing abstractions is *not* an automatic property of the brain. If all neurons were connected to all other neurons, then all the information of a situation would be retained— whether the information represents a general principle that occurs across many situations, or is unique to that situation. However, by slowly pruning its connections over childhood, the brain is able to eliminate the information that is unique to particular situations and focus on the information that occurs across many situations. This enables the brain to see commonalities between events and respond intelligently to new events based on their similarity to previously experienced events.

MAKING SENSE OF DEVELOPMENT

This role of environmental experience then reveals why it takes children so long to develop the ability to understand abstractions over childhood. Even though it would be more adaptive for infants to be born with the ability to understand abstractions, this does not happen because the brain *needs* environmental experience to understand abstractions. It is through exposure to many, many concrete instances of abstractions that the brain is given sufficient information to change the connections. Only once the connections are changed may abstractions be recognized and understood.

Consistent with this, it has been found that the ability to understand many abstractions such as advanced mathematical principles is a characteristic of formalized education.[101] In other words, exposure to schooling is what leads to the development of the ability to understand many abstractions. Natives from other cultures who are not given formalized education cannot understand these same abstractions, even though many adults exposed to a formalized education take them for granted.

However, this does not mean that natives from other cultures are incapable of understanding these abstractions. If the children of these natives are given a formalized education, they will also show the ability to understand these abstractions. So, again, the ability to understand abstractions is dependent on the environment.

ANOTHER LEARNING PROCESS IN THE BRAIN

It can also be seen that the process we have described whereby the neural connections are pruned through experience over childhood fits the definition of a learning process. After all, the term "learning" is commonly used to refer to the acquisition of knowledge through experience. The pruning process certainly depends on experience, and it leads to the acquisition of "knowledge" of the environment.

However, we can see that this learning process is different to many other situations that we typically take to be examples of learning, such as memorizing that the capital of France is Paris. We will be looking at this learning process in more detail in Chapter Six. For now, we can note that the above pruning process is different in a number of ways.[102]

First, the pruning process is a very slow or long-term learning process, because it depends on the neural connections actually changing their

98

physical structure. This retraction or extension of neural connections can take days, months, or even years to occur. It is not consistent with what we typically think of as learning, which occurs very rapidly—often, we can recall information such as the capital of France *immediately* after being told it for the *first* time. Rather, a pruning process that takes months or even years to show itself in terms of differences in behavior is consistent with the gradual development of the ability to understand abstractions that occurs over childhood.

Second, it is dependent on a limited supply of growth factor. This leads to the neural connections competing to form connections, and a consequent pruning of the connections that are not sufficiently reinforced. This, along with the slowness of the process, is supportive of finding elements in common across situations such as abstractions. It is not supportive of other learning occasions where it is more useful to store and remember as many details as possible. For instance, imagine being told that the capital of France is Paris, but then typically only hearing the location Paris, France. The word "capital" is often not used when referring to the location of Paris. If our memory for knowledge was due to the same abstraction process outlined above, then repeatedly being presented with Paris and France together—but not the term "capital"—would result in us forgetting that Paris is actually the capital of France. We would just know that Paris and France go together, but not that one is the capital of the other.

So, learning in different situations involves learning types of information that are in some ways incompatible—either commonalities across situations, or precise details of a particular concrete situation. It turns out that the brain has developed specialized learning mechanisms for both types of information.[103]

Finally, the learning process responsible for the development of abstractions also differs in that it is not active throughout the lifespan. As noted above, the process whereby the connections are pruned to adult levels takes place over childhood. Some regions, such as those responsible for processing visual and auditory information, reach adult levels at five years of age. Other regions undergo this pruning process for longer. However, by maturity, even these regions have ceased to perform this process.[104] It is also found that the growth cones responsible for the pruning of the neural connections over childhood are not found in the adult brain.[105]

This explains why the ability to understand abstractions increases over childhood, but does not increase in adulthood. It is also consistent with the finding that adults who engage in intellectually-demanding occupations and pastimes in adulthood do not show the same increase in the ability to understand abstractions that is a characteristic of childhood.

So, the pruning process we have described above would seem to be essential for the brain to learn abstractions. But how can this process be used to explain differences in intelligence?

CHAPTER FIVE

USING BRAIN SCIENCE TO EXPLAIN DIFFERENCES IN THE ABILITY TO UNDERSTAND

Initially, it would seem easy to use the pruning process described in the previous chapter to explain differences in the ability to understand. Since the pruning process depends on environmental stimulation, differences in the ability to understand would presumably be due to differences in environmental stimulation. In other words, if some children do not receive appropriate environmental stimulation when young, this would impair their ability to understand abstractions. However, this solution is not satisfactory for a number of reasons.

First, in Chapter Two we reviewed evidence supporting substantial heritability of differences in IQ. If differences in intelligence were simply due to differences in the environment, it would be expected that adopted children's IQ would more closely mirror that of their adoptive parents than their biological parents. The Between-Family Environment is also found to diminish in importance over childhood, even though the Between-Family Environment would presumably be expected to be the best indicator of differences in environmental stimulation.

Second, when findings showing the importance of the environment for the developing brain were first published, this led to the hypothesis that poor performance on IQ tests was due to children not receiving appropriate environmental stimulation when very young. Early-childhood intervention studies were then developed that sought to give disadvantaged children the environmental stimulation that it was thought they were missing. However, the outcome of these early intervention studies have been disappointing. Typically, they did raise the IQ of participants to some extent. However, their effectiveness was much less than was hoped. The average increase was around 10 IQ points, while the typical spread of IQ in the population is around 80 points. In no way did participation in these programs lead to disadvantaged children becoming gifted.[106]

Clearly, there is more to the story than just the effect of the environment. So, how might we use brain science to understand differences in human intelligence?

WHAT IQ TELLS US

It turns out that much of the evidence for understanding the cause of differences in human intelligence is given by the concept of IQ itself. While differences in intelligence could have manifested themselves in many different ways, the fact that they are best described by IQ immediately allows us to reject some possible causes of intelligence. This idea is illustrated in Figure 7 and the Figure 8's.

Figure 7 is a repeat of Figure 3, which was presented at the end of Chapter Two. It shows what the results of IQ testing reveal. Bright children develop the ability to understand abstractions at a greater rate over childhood.

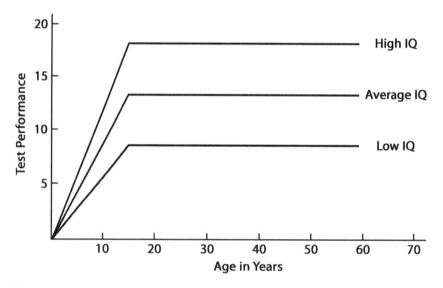

Figure 7. A repeat of Figure 3 showing what IQ testing tells us about how performance on intelligence tests changes over the lifespan for people who differ in intelligence.

Thought Experiments

We may then imagine what the curves would look like if differences in intelligence were due to various different causes. Figure 8A is what we would expect to observe if differences in intelligence were simply because of better memory. Because people of all ages are able to memorize information, you would then expect intelligence to keep increasing throughout both childhood and adulthood. Because this is not observed, we can reject the notion that differences in intelligence simply represent better memory or the ability to store information.

Figure 8B is like Figure 8A, but now there is a limit to the total amount of "useful" information that people can memorize. While there may be

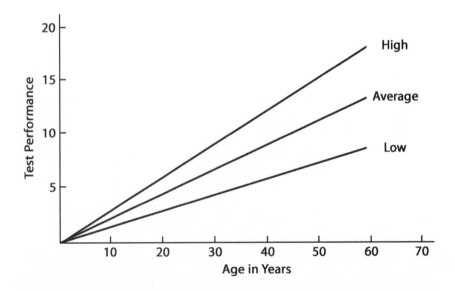

Figure 8A. A hypothetical illustration of how performance on intelligence tests would change over the lifespan if differences in intelligence simply reflected a better ability to memorize information.

other information to memorize, such as the population in Tunisia, it is unlikely to be useful in everyday life. Useful information would include basic facts that are frequently used. If this was the case, gifted people might still learn this information sooner. However, less-gifted people would eventually learn it as well—it would simply take them longer. In this case, there would be some maximum of performance, and gifted people would reach it sooner. The difference in intelligence would then be observed to decrease in later life, as less-gifted people would have more and more opportunity to learn the information. Again, this is not what is observed with differences in intelligence.

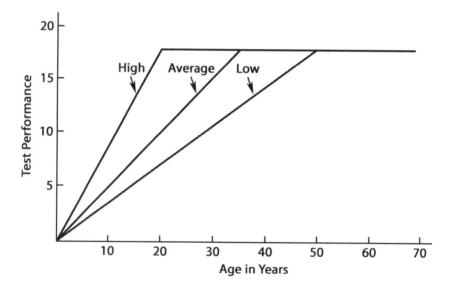

Figure 8B. A hypothetical illustration of how performance on intelligence tests would change over the lifespan if differences in intelligence reflected a better ability to memorize information, but there was also a limit to the total amount of useful information that may be memorized.

Figure 8C is what we would expect to observe if there was truly something different about the brains of gifted versus non-gifted individuals. For instance, what if gifted people had genes to give them a neural circuit that non-gifted people do not have, like some people get the gene to be able to roll their tongues and others do not? In this case, there would be some mental test that could be used to identify if someone is gifted at a young age. This very same mental test could then be used to identify giftedness at older ages as well. In other words, there is something fundamentally different between the brains of gifted and non-gifted people. However, again, this is not how differences in intelligence are observed.

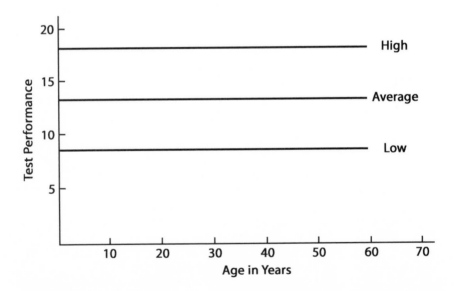

Figure 8C. A hypothetical illustration of how performance on intelligence tests would change over the lifespan if differences in intelligence were due to the presence of some brain structure or innate ability that does not change over the lifespan.

Figure 8D is where the development of intelligence is initially due to one process, such as the pruning of the connections we described in the previous chapter. However, once the connections are sufficiently developed to process the information correctly, some other factor then limits performance—such as speed of information processing or working memory capacity. This situation is indicated by an assessment of intelligence at a young age being unrelated to ultimate intellectual performance. Again, this is not what is observed. Instead, it is found that the speed at developing the ability to understand abstractions at an early age predicts the ability to understand more difficult abstractions at later ages.

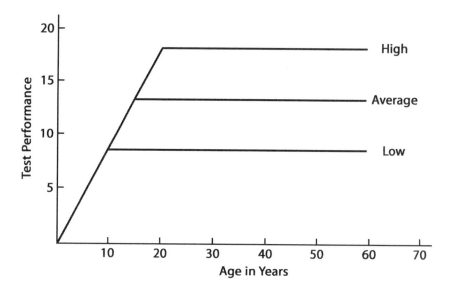

Figure 8D. A hypothetical illustration of how performance on intelligence tests would change if the process responsible for developing intelligence differed from the factor that leads to differences in intelligence in adulthood.

The essential point is that *none* of the illustrations shown in the Figure 8's describe what is observed when we look at differences in intelligence. Ever since IQ testing first began, it has been observed that differences in intellectual performance are best characterized by what is shown in Figure 7.

This tells us that people are smarter in adulthood because their ability to understand abstractions develops at a faster rate in childhood. This is the reason that IQ is used to represent differences in intelligence. If differences in intelligence were due to some other process, like one of the patterns shown in the Figure 8's, the "Intelligence Quotient"—whereby performance relative to age is used to describe intellectual performance—would not be used.

The use of IQ to represent differences in intelligence indicates that the process that is responsible for the development of abstractions over childhood also leads to differences in intelligence. However, we also saw in the previous chapter that the development of abstractions over childhood is likely due to the pruning of the neural connections in response to experience. This then suggests that there are differences in this process, and these differences lead to differences in intelligence. In other words, the fact that people differ in IQ indicates that *whatever process causes the increase in intelligence over childhood is also responsible for differences in intelligence in adulthood.*

Differences in Changing the Connections

This brings us to one of the most important concepts in this book. When the capacity of the brain to change its connections to the environment was first observed, it was just assumed that this process was the same for all individuals. However, what if this process is not the same in all individuals?[107]

For instance, imagine a child who is born with a brain that is very good at pruning its neural connections in response to the environment. Through experience, they would be able to develop the appropriate neural connections to understand the many abstractions or general principles that they experience in the environment. They would also do this more quickly than other children. In this way, they would seem to be more intellectually advanced for their age. They would appear "bright" or "gifted."

On the other hand, imagine a child who is born with a brain that is poorer at pruning to the environment. They would start off at the same point as the first child. However, when they are exposed to the same environment, they would develop the ability to understand abstractions at a slower rate.

In short, if children differed in their brain's ability to change the connections in response to the environment, you would get children developing at different rates—as reflected by IQ. Since different domains involve abstractions, and some brains are better at learning abstractions, you would also find that some children would be better across many tasks that involve abstractions. This would mean that their performance across different tasks would be correlated. In other words, you would find the general factor of intelligence, or g, that psychology has found.[108]

Despite this, as is shown in Figure 7, even children with relatively low intelligence do eventually develop the required neural connections for many abstractions. This indicates that the development of the ability to understand abstractions is due to some shaping mechanism. If a child has difficulty understanding a particular abstraction initially, the neural connections will keep on changing until they can eventually understand the abstraction—it just takes them longer. So, there is no fundamental limitation in the brain that places a ceiling on the performance of someone with a lower IQ.[109]

RETHINKING INTELLIGENCE

This turns out to be a revolutionary concept. When people hear that an adult possesses a high IQ, they typically assume that it means that the adult has "something" in their brain that enables them to solve problems.

For instance, take the abstraction problems like Raven's Progressive Matrices, Numbers Series, and Word Analogies that we saw in Chapter Two. These are problems that test takers have never seen before. It is then assumed that whatever factor leads someone to be intelligent must be active at the time a person is actually *given the test*, because this is the time at which they determine the correct answer. In other words, it is argued that a high-IQ person does better at an intelligence test because their brain possesses more of some characteristic such as greater speed of information processing or greater working memory capacity at the time they are taking the test. This characteristic is at a maximum in young adulthood because the ability to understand abstractions is at a maximum at this time.[110]

This implicit belief is also the underlying basis for believing in "quick fixes" to boost intelligence. If differences in intelligence were due to differences in how the brain processes information at the time a problem is being solved, then changes in the real-time processing capacity of the brain should be able to increase intelligence. Not surprisingly, there is a ready market for "smart pills" and simple exercises that it is believed will increase the ability to understand abstractions.

However, no such factor exists that is active in the adult brain! An adult understands an abstraction only because of the years of environmental experience that they accrued during childhood that led to the correct neural connections being developed to enable them to recognize or understand the abstraction. There is no shortcut for this process.

Once these neural connections are in place though, a person can recognize the abstraction in various contexts. This enables them to understand the abstraction not only at the time they learned it, but also when they are presented with it later—such as when doing an intelligence test.

We can see, then, that the abstraction problems are not really *novel* problems. A participant may never have seen the exact same problem before. However, if they are able to solve the problem, it will be because it involves abstractions that they are already familiar with and can understand. When you are in the process of solving one of these problems, you will likely think, "I know the abstraction or general principle I need to use here." In short, these problems do not involve forming a new abstraction. They involve recognizing abstractions that you already understand in different contexts.[111]

An adult with a high IQ has a high IQ because they have developed many different neural circuits over childhood that are specialized for recognizing or understanding different abstractions. It is the possession of these different neural circuits that enables them to do well on different tasks that involve understanding abstractions.[112]

WHY IS IT SO DIFFICULT TO INCREASE INTELLIGENCE?

This then raises another issue. It is being argued that giving children the right environmental experiences will lead to them being able to understand abstractions. However, anyone familiar with the psychological literature will know that attempts to increase intelligence in childhood through environmental experience often meet with disappointing results. This includes the early intervention programs that were discussed at the beginning of this chapter.[113]

Why has it been so difficult to raise intelligence through environmental interventions? Obviously, using environmental stimulation to raise the intelligence of children with low IQs is problematic if the reason they have low IQs is because their brain is not effective at adapting to environmental stimulation in the first place. However, there are also other reasons why intelligence could seem to be so insensitive to environmental interventions.

A Slow Process

As we have already noted, the pruning process responsible for abstractions involves physically changing the neural connections. These changes do not happen quickly. It can take months or even years for environmental stimulation to actually change the connections of the neurons. This is unlike what we normally think of as learning, where differences in behavior can be observed immediately following a learning experience.

Months or years of experience may be needed not only because of the slow speed at which the brain can change its neural connections, but also because the child might need to receive hundreds or even thousands of concrete instances of the abstraction. These examples might be needed to give the child's brain enough information to develop the connections to gradually extract out the general principles that exist across the many concrete instances. So it is helpful that the neural connections take considerable time to change. If the neural connections could change quickly, then each individual concrete instance would be learned—but the general or underlying principle would be missed.

This means that environmental stimulation would not have an immediate effect on the ability to understand, and would give the appearance that the intervention has not been effective.[114] Indeed, it is found that intervention programs are more effective the longer a program runs.[115]

This account is also consistent with another characteristic of intervention studies. With these studies, it is often found that a child's IQ is raised while they are a part of the program. However, this IQ gain is gradually lost once the child leaves the program.[116]

This suggests that enhanced stimulation does accelerate the child's intellectual development while they are a part of the program. However, once the program is over, the amount of stimulation they receive falls back to pre-intervention levels. Their rate of intellectual development would then also fall back to what it was prior to the program. More-gifted children who were not a part of the program could then catch up and re-overtake them, causing the intervention participants' IQ to fall back to what it was originally.

This tells us that environmental interventions do aid the development of intelligence. However, it is difficult to create a massive change in the amount of stimulation a child receives. An intervention that consists of only a couple of extra hours of experience per week is insufficient. Rather, interventions need to be as intensive as possible. Also, rather than only being a temporary program, such as in early childhood, they should be in place throughout the entire period in which children are able to increase their ability to understand abstractions.

Abstractions Depend on other Abstractions

Another reason that it can be difficult to teach abstractions is that understanding many abstractions depend on understanding other underlying abstractions first. As an adult, since the understanding of abstractions seems obvious, it can be easy to overlook that the underlying abstractions also needed to be learned.

For instance, it is not possible to teach a five-year-old child algebra. This is at least partly because, before understanding algebra, they need to understand other abstractions such as numbers and arithmetic. Just teaching these underlying abstractions so that the child has the underlying principles necessary for algebra takes many years, so it is not feasible to teach a five-year-old algebra.

Again, the development of understanding is a long-term process. This can make it seem as though it does not depend on environmental stimulation since short-term environmental stimulation has limited effect.

Timing Differences across Brain Regions

Another reason, as was described in the previous chapter, is that different areas in the brain undergo the pruning process at different times during childhood. The visual area adapts the connections up until five years of age. On the other hand, areas that represent higher abstractions may not go through the pruning process until later in childhood. This means that it is not possible to teach a child higher abstractions until the appropriate brain region is going through the pruning process.

However, once the area has reached the time when it is open to environmental stimulation, it is environmental experience that shapes the neural connections and enables the child to understand the relevant abstractions.

So, evidence that children cannot learn something through environmental intervention at a particular age does not disprove the importance of environmental stimulation at another age. Rather, there should be a match between when a particular brain region is going through the pruning process and when a child is being given appropriate environmental experiences.

Examples of Environmental Influence

Despite the difficulties sometimes encountered with attempts to raise intelligence, is there convincing evidence that the ability to understand is dependent on environmental experience? It turns out that there is!

Recall that tests used to assess intelligence such as Raven's Progressive Matrices involve presenting participants with a configuration of elements that they have never seen before. General principles or abstractions place restrictions on what the possible answer to the problem is, and participants need to use these general principles or abstractions to determine the correct answer. However, these characteristics do not *just* apply to the tests of abstraction we have already discussed. There are other examples where the influence of the environment is more clear.

Mathematics

Consider mathematical reasoning. Mathematical reasoning reflects exactly the same process. Participants are presented with a new configuration of elements. They must then apply particular abstractions in order to determine the correct answer.

For instance, consider the problem "Jane has eight walnuts. She gives half of her walnuts to Mark. Mark then eats two walnuts. How many walnuts does Mark have left?" While you have solved mathematical problems before, it is unlikely that you have seen this exact problem. Not only are the names and objects different, but the process that determines how many walnuts Mark has left is also distinct. And yet, humans are able to solve these problems. This is because they can apply abstractions that they have learned such as "half" and "subtract" to new situations. For this reason, problems like these are essentially identical to the abstraction tests we have already discussed.

Consistent with this, the ability to solve mathematical problems like this is related to the other tests of abstraction that we have described.[117] In other words, children who are good at identifying the abstractions involved in Raven's Progressive Matrices are also good at identifying the abstractions required to solve mathematical problems. This indicates that the same brain mechanism is employed in both situations.

We can then ask—do children need to be taught mathematical principles? Or can they perform these computations without being given appropriate environmental experience? Surprisingly, even the staunchest advocate for a genetic view of intelligence would not deny the need to be taught these principles. Children are given extensive experience at school with these types of problems because they *need* this experience to be able to learn them.[118] This indicates that the abstractions used to solve these problems are based on experience, or a learning process.

Language and Literacy

Similar arguments can be made for the role of the environment when language and literacy are considered. Again, both language development and the speed of acquiring literacy skills are early indicators of giftedness.[119] However, both the language a child acquires and their literacy skills vary based on the language that they were exposed to as a child.

For example, a child who is born in China grows up with the ability to speak Chinese and to write using Chinese characters. If that same child is born in the USA, they do not still grow up with the ability to speak and write Chinese. We take it for granted that different languages are spoken around the world, but this is actually telling us that much of language is not innate, but based on environmental experience.

And since gifted children learn language skills faster, it means that they can learn the required language structures faster no matter what they are—once again indicating that intelligence is about learning regularities or patterns in the environment.

Tests of Abstraction

However, what about the tests of abstraction themselves? Are the abstractions involved in these tests dependent on environmental experience?

We can observe that the abstractions involved in Word Analogies and Number Series are without a doubt dependent on environmental experience. Since performance on these tests is related to performance on the Raven's Progressive Matrices, it follows that the ability to understand the abstractions used in the Raven's Progressive Matrices are also dependent on environmental experience for their development.

This is credible, as even Raven's Progressive Matrices involves abstractions that are characteristic of the environment. These include number, symmetry, and treating elements of a compound independently. Children experience these abstractions while growing up. Indeed, as was shown in the previous chapter, kittens cannot perceive horizontal lines if they are not given experience with them during infancy. Since even the simplest abstractions involved in Raven's Progressive Matrices are much more abstract than horizontal lines, it is likely that the ability to perceive these abstractions depends on learning rather than being an innate feature of the brain.

EXPLAINING THE HERITABILITY

The above arguments suggest that there are very good reasons to believe that the development of the ability to understand abstractions is due to environmental experience. How do we then explain the heritability shown by intelligence?

Remember that heritability is referring to whether genes are causing *differences* in a characteristic. If the environment is important for the development of a characteristic but everyone receives the same environment, then the heritability of that characteristic will be very high. In other words, even though the environment is essential for the characteristic's development, genes will be responsible for differences across people in the characteristic.[120]

However, is this explanation really sufficient to account for the heritability shown by intelligence? Surely there are large differences in the environment across people. Why are these large differences in the environment not reflected by intelligence having lower heritability? It turns out that there is more to the story. Here, again, it gets a bit more complicated.

g Loadings

Psychologists interested in intelligence will not deny that experience plays a crucial role in developing the ability to understand abstractions in mathematics and language. However, they will argue that you should not be looking at these tasks to assess the heritability of intelligence. Instead, you should be looking at *highly g-loaded tasks*.

What are highly *g*-loaded tasks? Recall that psychologists observed that performance on different intellectual tasks is correlated. This means that people who perform well on one intellectual task also do well on other intellectual tasks. The concept of a general factor of intelligence, or *g*, is used to account for this. The notion is that some people are higher in this factor, and this allows them to do well on all tasks that depend on this *g* factor. A major goal of psychologists, then, is to discover what this *g* factor is.

However, it turns out that not all intellectual performances are equally correlated with each other. Some intellectual performances have only low correlations with other intellectual performances, while others have much higher correlations.

It is argued that intellectual performances with low correlations are measuring something that is unique to those particular tasks—rather than an underlying ability that is responsible for performances across many tasks. If the task was more dependent on the common underlying ability, then correlations with the other intellectual tasks would be higher. Therefore, psychologists focus their investigation on intellectual tasks that show high correlations with other tasks. These tasks are what are meant by *highly g-loaded tasks*.

So, when researchers assess the heritability of intelligence, they are not referring to the heritability of all intellectual abilities. Instead, they are only referring to a subset of intellectual abilities—those that have high *g* loadings.[121]

What Tasks Have High g Loadings?

Assessing tasks that have high *g* loadings would initially seem to make sense. These tasks would seem to be characteristic of the underlying *g* factor that contributes to performance across all mental ability tasks. However, let us see what happens if intelligence is due to a learning process like that described above.

According to the above framework, there would not be abilities that are more or less dependent on some "general factor" for their successful performance. All abstractions would develop as a result of the same adaptation or learning process, so tasks with high g loadings would not be special in this respect.

However, astute readers will realize that you would still get some abilities that correlate more with each other than others. These would be abilities that have the *smallest differences in environmental experience across individuals.*

To better understand this, remember that a correlation is said to occur between two abilities if people who are high on one are high on the other as well. Similarly, people who are low on one are also low on the other. In other words, performance on one measure can be predicted from performance on the other measure.

Imagine, then, abilities where all children receive the required environmental experience. Examples would include basic visual patterns, simple number concepts, and words used to describe common relationships in the environment.

A child whose brain is better at adapting the neural connections to the environment will be better at all of these abilities. They have received the appropriate stimulation, and their brain is able to adapt and extract out the commonalities or abstractions. On the other hand, a person whose brain is not as efficient at adapting its connections will be lower at all of these abilities despite the same environmental experience. Since the same individuals will be either high or low performers across all of these tasks, these different tasks will show high correlations with each other.

Imagine, on the other hand, abilities where there are large differences in environmental experience across individuals. This would include tasks where some children express an interest in the task and study it intensely, while other children either are not interested in it or do not get much exposure to it.

In this case, a person whose brain is better at adapting the neural connections to the environment may *not* be better across all of the tasks. They may have taken an interest in one task and consequently been exposed to relevant environmental experiences that allow their brain to learn the abstractions that are present. For another task, they may not have received the necessary stimulation to learn about the underlying abstractions. In this case, we can see that people who are high performers in one task will not necessarily be high performers in other tasks as well. The correlations between the tasks would be lower.

When psychologists are interested in intelligence, we have noted that they assess tasks that have high *g* loadings. These are the former tasks, where the correlations are higher.

But wait… The reason that these tasks are highly correlated is because children get *similar* environmental experiences. If they get similar environmental experiences, then whatever differences in performance exist would be determined by the relative ability of the brain to adapt its neural connections to the environment. Since this process involves biochemical and physiological processes, it is likely coded by the genes. So differences in performance on these tasks would be largely determined by the genes and not differences in the environment. They would show *high heritability*.

121

This means that these tasks have high g loadings not because they are more representative of intelligence—they have high g loadings just because children get similar environmental experiences with which to develop these particular abilities in the current environment. However, choosing to use these tasks to then assess the heritability of intelligence overall would exaggerate the effects of the genes. In contrast, using tasks with lower g loadings would lead to lower estimates of heritability.

This is a complex argument, but a mathematical model can easily show its validity.[122] The key point is that intelligence can show high heritability while still depending on environmental experience to develop it. Even more support for this argument comes from the observation that the g loadings of different intellectual tasks are found to be directly related to their heritability![123]

THE EVOLUTION OF UNDERSTANDING

We can now turn to consider the role that evolution has played in our ability to understand. Some researchers have attempted to use evolutionary principles to account for specific aspects of human intelligence. In other words, since our genes evolved in a hunter-gatherer environment, it is argued that the abilities we display in our current environment are actually abilities that evolved in and were suited to a hunter-gatherer society.[124]

Hopefully, readers can see a flaw with this type of argument. Humans are distinctive because of our extreme flexibility in dealing with different environments and situations—including ones that are far removed from the hunter-gatherer environment from which our genes evolved. This includes our ability to create machines such as computers, transform our environment to make it more habitable, and form social structures that have enabled advanced civilization.

Humans show this flexibility by understanding general principles or rules that apply across situations. We then use these principles and rules to guide our behavior—not only in previously experienced situations, but also in newer situations for which we do not have direct experience. Often these principles are specialized for our modern environment and society.

Is it plausible to suggest that these general principles could have evolved in a hunter-gatherer environment? Or to put it more directly, what use could the ability to perceive the next number in a series have been in an environment concerned with gathering food and hunting wild animals? What about the ability to design new architecture, or create electronic devices?

Researchers who advocate the importance of the hunter-gatherer environment for human intelligence are notable, then, because they do not provide any serious explanation of how our modern understandings could have served a purpose in a hunter-gatherer society. It is merely claimed that they would be.

In contrast, this book is arguing that each individual understanding or ability is not based on an independently evolved neural circuit. As we saw in the previous chapter, the capacity of the brain to reorganize itself following injury also disproves this view. Instead, evolution has led to a general brain-adaptation mechanism that enables any underlying structure in the environment to be learned and understood.

This general mechanism would have been useful in a hunter-gatherer environment for avoiding predators, gathering food, and basic tool use. However, as our society has become more sophisticated, it has enabled humans to understand many environmental challenges that were not present in our evolutionary past. In this way, humans can adapt and behave appropriately, not only in a hunter-gatherer environment, but also in our modern technological society. It also means that our evolutionary environment has limited relevance for understanding modern human intellectual abilities.

Difference to Primates

The adaptation of the neural connections to the environment can also account for the massive increase in intelligence that has occurred in humans compared with primates. As has already been noted, there is little difference between humans and primates in terms of genetic material—as little as 500 genes. This makes it unlikely that genes directly code for all of the differences in intelligence that exist between humans and primates. This is especially true since these genetic differences must also be responsible for the obvious physical differences between humans and primates.

What has changed between humans and primates is the size of the cerebral cortex. This is the brain region whose connections are especially sensitive to the environment over childhood. However, there may be more to the difference between humans and primates than this. It is also observed that humans seem to be more like infant primates than adult primates.[125] Normally, taking on the characteristics of an infant would be disadvantageous, but the infant brain in primates is also more adaptable to the environment. If humans are more like infant primates, this implies that our brains will also be more adaptive to the environment.

Indeed, as has already been stated, if the development of the ability to understand was due to a genetic process, then evolutionary pressures would lead to a speeding up of the development of understanding over childhood. Infants would be born already possessing a high ability to understand. However, if environmental experience is required to understand, infants should be born with less inbuilt mechanisms. This enables the environment to maximize its effect on the development of understanding.

How Understanding Develops

We have examined evidence indicating that the ability to understand abstractions develops through a learning process that changes the neural connections during childhood. Do psychologists who study child development find this?

Answering this question has been surprisingly difficult. The problem is similar to the difficulty in directly assessing the contribution of genes and environment to human intelligence. Ethically, it is not possible to take children and randomly assign them to groups that are treated differently in childhood—so we cannot see the direct effect of the environment on child development. Instead, developmental psychologists typically need to look at how intelligence develops under normal circumstances. They then try to determine whether this development is due to experience.

The most famous developmental psychologist was Jean Piaget. He argued that during childhood, two fundamental processes were at work that led to a child's increasing understanding and knowledge of the world. He termed these processes *assimilation* and *accommodation*.

Assimilation involves the process of fitting reality into a person's current way of thinking. When people experience something new, he argued that there is a degree of "bending" or distorting of the experience as they form mental representations to represent the experience based on what they can understand.

However, if the child's understanding is not a good fit for what they are experiencing, Piaget argued that *accommodation* would occur. This was a gradual process involving adjustments in thinking resulting from the demands of reality. The organization of thought would be modified so as to lead to a different and more satisfactory assimilation of the experience. In this way, the child's internal experience or representation of the environment would change over time and become a better fit with reality. Piaget also stressed that children would move to increasingly abstract representations over the course of childhood.

Readers are likely to note the obvious similarities between Piaget's account and what brain science now tells us about brain development. Assimilation would represent a child's initial understanding of an event based on the neural connections that are currently in their brain. Accommodation would then represent the process whereby these neural connections gradually change over time, extracting better commonalities to represent a better understanding of environmental experiences.

So Piaget argued that it was experience that leads to children's increasing ability to abstract over childhood. These abstractions would enable the child to better understand the occurrence of events based on underlying principles, rather than events seeming to be just unrelated occurrences.

The Effect of Schooling

Given the importance of experience for developing understanding, where would children obtain this experience? Presumably, the major source is schooling. We can then ask what effect schooling has on the development of the ability to understand.

Clearly, children learn many abstractions at school. Mathematical and scientific principles are just some examples. This is sufficient to show that the ability to understand abstractions is dependent on experience.

However, much of the focus of the effect of schooling on intelligence has been on IQ. This is problematic as IQ tests were originally designed to measure indicators of giftedness that were the least affected by the amount or quality of schooling that children received—so we would expect schooling to have a minimal effect. Even so, we can still evaluate the effect of schooling on IQ.

To begin with, it is found that there is a large correlation in adulthood between number of years of school attended and IQ.[126] However, such a correlation does not establish causation. It is quite possible that children attend school for longer because they are more intelligent.

What is really needed is an experiment where children are randomly allocated to different groups, and these groups are given different amounts of schooling. However, again for ethical reasons, such an experiment has not been undertaken. Researchers have thus had to resort to other circumstances to try and infer the role of schooling on IQ.[127]

One approach has been to examine the effect of the cutoff age when children enter school.[128] Since schooling is based on a calendar year, children will start school either relatively younger or relatively older than their classmates. This means that we can study the effect of up to a year of schooling on children of the same age. When this is done, it is found that children who have received more schooling are more advanced. This effect was observed not just in the amount of knowledge acquired, but also in their ability to understand abstractions. This indicates that schooling does improve intelligence.[129]

Similarly, children who are prevented from attending school due to factors beyond their control are found to be impaired in IQ performance.[130] For instance, in the 1960s, some schools in Virginia were closed for several years as a protest against school integration. Children who did not receive a formal education during this time were estimated to have suffered a decline in IQ of about 6 points for each year of school missed. Similar findings have been reported for children who were prevented from attending school during the Second World War.

It has also been found that gypsy children show similar IQ performance to that of other children until they reach school age. However, once the other children begin school, it is found that the IQ of gypsy children steadily declines.[131] This again indicates that the ability to understand abstractions depends on environmental experience.

The Flynn Effect

Another finding that indicates the effect of the environment is the Flynn effect. The Flynn effect refers to the finding that performance on IQ tests has been gradually improving over the last century. In other words, an average 20-year-old now will do better on an intelligence test compared to how an average 20-year-old from the 1950s did on the same intelligence test. This increase has been estimated at around 3 IQ points per decade. The effect is named after James Flynn, who was the researcher who first observed the phenomenon.[132]

This finding again goes against a strictly genetic view of intelligence. The pool of genes that makes up the human DNA would not have changed over the last few generations—it takes many, many generations of selective breeding for evolution to change the relative occurrence of genes in the gene pool. This means that the increase in test performance must be due to changes in the environment over the last century.

Even more interestingly, an alternative explanation of the Flynn effect is simply an increase in knowledge over time. In short, children might be exposed to more information now than they were in past generations. Recalling this information then helps them on IQ tests. If this was true, it would be predicted that performance on subtests within an IQ test that depend mainly on memorizing information should show the greatest increases.

In fact, researchers have found the opposite.[133] Performance on intelligence tests that depend the least on memorized information and the most on understanding abstractions show the greatest increases. This includes performance on the Raven's Progressive Matrices, a test that requires very little "knowledge" in order to solve the problems.

There is also evidence that increased environmental stimulation during childhood is responsible for the Flynn effect. For instance, schooling has improved in quality over the last few decades. This includes both the number of years children spend in school, and a change from a system that emphasizes rote learning to a system that emphasizes understanding. It has been argued that these changes have caused the Flynn effect.[134] Television and video games are also speculated to play a role.[135]

Increase in Intelligence across History

However, what if we look at intelligence not just over the last few decades, but over the course of history? Has intelligence increased over this time?

It can be observed that humans have indeed become smarter over the centuries. Aristotle (384 BC–322 BC) is one of the most famous philosophers in history. And yet, his notion of physics consisted of breaking the world down into just five elements—fire, earth, air, water, and ether. A typical present-day college student would immediately reject such a notion. The ability to perceive the underlying patterns that exist in the world is now much more sophisticated.

Similarly, calculus was originally understood by few but the most esteemed thinkers, such as Isaac Newton. Now, it is a part of the high-school syllabus. Even as recently as the beginning of the twentieth century, researchers were publishing quaint theories such as the relationship between body mass and personality.[136] Their writings also reveal a lack of sophistication compared with today's researchers.[137]

All of these examples involve the comprehension or understanding of abstractions. They fit the criterion that defines tests that are used to assess intelligence today—namely applying general principles in new contexts. We can also see that they depend on the environment for their acquisition. Once again, this indicates the importance of the environment for the development of intelligence.

The Final Nail in the Coffin

We have observed that differences in intelligence represent differences in the ability to understand abstractions. Understanding abstractions are dependent on retaining information that is relevant to the abstraction, and filtering out information that is unique to specific concrete instances of the abstraction. We have also observed that the brain prunes its neural connections over childhood in response to experience. It is argued that this process leads to the ability to recognize and understand abstractions.

IQ is used to represent intelligence because people develop the ability to understand abstractions at different rates over childhood. This indicates that the process by which abstractions are learned is also responsible for differences in intelligence. This chapter has shown that many findings associated with IQ and human intelligence can be accounted for using such an approach. Some brains are better at changing their connections, and this enables a better understanding of many abstractions to be developed.

However, is there direct evidence that differences in the pruning process described in the previous chapter is responsible for differences in intelligence? It turns out that there is!

Due to their small size, looking at the precise neural connections in humans while they are alive is not possible. This has led to difficulties in identifying brain characteristics that are related to intelligence. However, the pruning process that occurs in the cerebral cortex results in such a massive loss of neural connections that the entire volume of the cerebral cortex can change. This volume change can be measured using MRI.

Philip Shaw and colleagues at the National Institute of Health then conducted a study whereby the volume of the cerebral cortex in children was monitored over childhood. It was found that there was no relationship between cortical volume and IQ. However, it was found that the *change* in cortical volume over childhood was related! High IQ children would develop more connections initially. They would then go through a much more rigorous pruning process during childhood.[138] This confirms that differences in changing the connections over childhood underlie differences in the ability to understand abstractions.

Chapter Six

How the Brain Produces Human Intelligence

Wе have so far identified the brain process that leads to the ability to understand abstractions. However, there is more to human intelligence than abstraction. As we have already discussed, adults of all ages possess the ability to memorize new information. Chapter Two showed how crystallized knowledge or facts and expertise continue to increase throughout most of the lifespan.

This chapter will focus on how this memory process works, and how it and abstraction combine to produce human intelligence. We will then consider how normal human intelligence differs from other examples of exceptional behavior. Finally, we will look at what understanding really means.

WHAT IS MEMORY?

When we use the term memory, we typically use it to refer to the storing or memorizing of information that we can recall later. One example is the memorization of facts.[139] We can learn that the capital of France is Paris, and that the population of Brazil is 200 million. If you are then asked what the capital of France is, or the population of Brazil, you can answer correctly.

The only way to know the answers to these questions is if you have been previously given this information. This is unlike tests of abstraction, where you are unlikely to have been told the correct answer before, but you can work out the answer by using general principles.

There are a number of additional differences between learning facts and learning abstractions. For instance, facts can be learned very quickly. Often, people are able to remember that the capital of France is Paris after being told this information only *once*. In contrast, abstractions are very difficult to learn. They can take months or even years of appropriate experiences. Another characteristic of good memory is storing as many details as possible. In contrast, abstraction involves ignoring information.

Recalling facts also feels different to abstract reasoning. In an abstract reasoning problem, we can "see" what the correct answer is. The correct answer seems to be the only one that fits. We *know* it to be true. This is because the neural connections have adapted so that this is the only pattern of neural firings that the neural connections allow. Even if we have not used the abstraction for years, it still comes automatically, without effort, and seems obvious. The examples of abstraction problems in Chapter Two show these characteristics. If you are told that the answer to the first sample Raven's problem is D, or the answer to the second Raven's problem is B, can you "see" this?

On the other hand, when asked what the capital of France is, the answer just seems to "pop" into our head. The answer may be very familiar and this familiarity leads to a sense that it is correct, but you cannot "see" that it is necessarily correct. In some cases, we can only remember fragments and the memory is rusty or hazy—but by spending time, the memory can gradually come back to us. You might remember that the capital of France starts with "P" but not recall the complete name. At other times, the information can elude us completely and we know that it is lost. Our memory for facts or knowledge is fragile, and forgetting is common.

Our memory for facts may also be quickly overwritten or replaced. For instance, the Indian city of Bombay was renamed Mumbai in 1996. If you are told that the new name for Bombay is Mumbai, you can then recall the name Mumbai instead of Bombay when asked about this city.

Other examples of memory include remembering what you ate on your birthday, memorizing a mathematical formula, and remembering how to send an email. Learning a new word is also an example of this memory, assuming that you can understand what the new word means. Learning the new word involves associating the word or symbol with the meaning that you can understand. Hearing the word then recalls the meaning.

Memory in the Brain

When we begin to look at the neural basis of memory, an area of the brain known as the hippocampus and surrounding areas is found to be important. The importance of this area was amply demonstrated by the case of HM (identified as Henry Gustav Molaison after his death) in the 1950s.[140]

HM suffered from intractable epilepsy. This meant that a region of his brain would start firing uncontrollably, leading to a seizure. Doctors determined that the region of the brain that was causing the uncontrollable firing was the hippocampus, an area located near the center of the brain.

It was decided that the best course of action would be to remove the hippocampus and nearby structures surgically. Doctors hoped that this would eliminate the seizures, and yet have minimal impact on HM's intellectual functioning. This belief was based on past operations on other patients that suggested that removing specific regions of the brain did not severely impact intellectual functioning.

After the surgery, HM's seizures were reduced. However, the surgery also had a drastic effect on HM's memory. It was found that he suffered from profound *anterograde amnesia*. This indicated that HM was unable to form new memories.

It is difficult to comprehend just what it would have been like to have been HM after the surgery. It was found that he could still think normally, but he could not commit any of his thoughts to memory so they could be recalled later on. This meant that he could engage in conversation with someone but, the next day, he would not remember meeting them. Indeed, if he was talking to someone and his thoughts were distracted, he would then look back at the person and not know who they were or what they had been talking about. His inability to form new memories meant that he continued to think it was the 1950s decades later.[141]

This case, as well as animal studies, have indicated that the hippocampus and associated regions form a crucial part of our ability to store information rapidly.[142] The hippocampus has extensive connections with neurons throughout the cerebral cortex. This means that the hippocampus gets information from the "thinking" parts of the brain.

The connections in the hippocampus itself also differ from the connections in the other parts of the brain. The connections do not go through the growth and pruning process that leads to the major changes in the connections that we described in Chapter Four. However, the connections can rapidly change their efficiency. This change in strength can occur after only a single trial or exposure, permitting the fast memorization of information.[143]

How Memory Works

Researchers have found that neurons in the hippocampus form what is described as an *auto-associative network*.[144] Essentially, the neurons are wired up so that they can associate patterns with themselves. If a configuration or sequence of inputs is sent to the hippocampus, it will recall the *same* configuration or sequence of inputs.

At first, this does not sound that interesting or useful. However, the true power of auto-associative networks comes from what happens once they have learned a given configuration or pattern. Once they have learned it, they need to be given only *part* of the configuration or pattern, and the auto-associative network will then fill in or complete the rest. Figure 9 shows how an auto-associative network can be presented with a picture. Later, it is presented with only a fragment of that picture. Given this fragment, it is able to recall the complete picture from memory!

Train the auto-associative network by presenting it with an image of a puppy.	After training, present the auto-associative network with only a part of the original image.	The auto-associative network will then reproduce the original image of the puppy.

Figure 9. An illustration of how an auto-associative network can learn a configuration of elements and then recall this configuration later when prompted by only some of the original elements.

Again, this may not sound that interesting or useful. However, just think about how your own memory works. If you are told that the capital of France is Paris, the auto-associative network in your brain would store the configuration of capital-France-Paris. If someone asks you later what the capital of France is, what would the auto-associative network do? It would be presented with a part of the configuration, capital-France. It would then complete it—causing the answer of Paris to pop into your head!

This basic principle fits other examples of memory as well. For your birthday, you ate pizza and cake. This is a configuration. If you then think of your birthday, your auto-associative network will recall the pizza and cake. If you think of a type of mathematical problem, your auto-associative network can recall the exact formula. If you think of sending an email, your auto-associative network can recall the steps you need to go through.

These brief examples show just how useful and powerful an auto-associative network is. The ability to store configurations or sequences of elements and then recall them based on only a subset of the elements is an ability that we use all the time.[145]

ABSTRACTION AND MEMORY

So, if an auto-associative network is so useful, this raises the question—why doesn't human intelligence consist of just an auto-associative network? Why has the human brain evolved the capacity to learn abstractions as well?

The answer to this question was given in Chapter One. Suppose that the human brain consisted of *only* an auto-associative network. This auto-associative network received input directly from the senses. This includes receptors in the eyes that convey information about light, and receptors in the ears that convey information about sound. It is this information that is used to form configurations or patterns.

Imagine, then, that you read that the capital of France is Paris. If someone asks you what the *capital* of *France* is, you would be unable to answer. The original information is written text, while the question is spoken words. The spoken words cannot retrieve the pattern based on written text, because they are from a different pattern—so hearing the words *capital* and *France* would not enable the completion of the pattern that was learned when it was read that the capital of France is Paris.

In short, while an auto-associative network is potentially very useful, by itself it is also quite limited in the extent to which the patterns it learns can generalize to other relevant situations. This reflects rote memorization.

On the other hand, imagine if the auto-associative network does not take input directly from the senses, but takes input from information

139

that has already been abstracted. This information can generalize across situations.

In the example just given, when we read that the capital of France is Paris, we do not store images of the words capital-France-Paris. We store mental representations of the words *capital-France-Paris*. Either seeing or hearing these words leads to the same mental representations. This way, our auto-associative network can complete the pattern when we are later questioned with either written or spoken words.

This can be illustrated by asking yourself how you found out that the capital of France is Paris. Did a woman tell you? Was it a man? Did you read it in a book? Typically, you cannot remember, because your brain did not store all of this information. Only information that generalizes across situations was stored.

Solving Abstraction Problems

Let us now return to the tests of abstraction that we examined in Chapter Two. These tests were the Raven's Progressive Matrices, Word Analogies, and Number Series. As already described, these tests are known to be good predictors of performance in situations that reflect the special capabilities of the human brain. This includes performance at school and college, as well as intellectually-challenging occupations such as being a doctor or an engineer. Since performance on these tasks is related to successful performance in these situations, it suggests that understanding these tasks should be a *key* goal if we are to understand how the human brain is able to be special.

We can then see that each of these tests involve two processes—the ability to extract abstractions, and the ability to store and recall sequences or configurations of these extracted abstractions. Using these processes results in successfully solving these problems.

Let us begin with the Raven's Progressive Matrices. For the middle item that involves parallel lines, solving the problem requires abstracting out the number of items in each element. The number of items going from left to right is 1, 2, 3 for the top row and 1, 2, 3 for the second row. The final row then gives 1, 2. Based on pattern completion, if an auto-associative network has been previously presented with 1, 2, 3 and 1, 2, 3, and is then presented with 1, 2, it will produce 3 as the answer.

If we go down the columns, we can abstract out the angles. The first column is vertical, diagonal, horizontal. The second column is vertical, diagonal, horizontal. The third column starts with vertical, diagonal. An auto-associative network with pattern completion would recall horizontal to complete the pattern. So based on identifying the underlying abstractions and using an auto-associative network to store those abstractions, the prediction for the missing item would be 3 horizontal. This corresponds to the correct answer.

This indicates that a system that has learned to extract abstractions and can store configurations of these abstractions can solve Raven's Progressive Matrices problems. In fact, not only can it solve these problems, but Raven's Progressive Matrices seems as if it was designed to assess such a system.

What, then, about Word Analogies? We can again see that the ability to extract abstractions and learn configurations of these abstractions would enable successful performance on these items.

Let us consider the first word analogy. Puppy is to Dog as Kitten is to *Cat*. Learning the meaning of words is due to our auto-associative network. It involves learning a pattern or configuration that involves both the symbol for the word and what the word represents. The symbol for the word can then retrieve the meaning, and the meaning can retrieve the symbol.

If we can understand abstractions associated with the word, these abstractions then become part of the meaning. For instance, young animals grow into "adult" animals, irrespective of the specific animal involved. So someone who understands this abstraction would not only memorize a Dog as being the same animal as a Puppy, but also an "adult" version. Similarly, they would memorize a Cat as being an "adult" version of a Kitten. The same "adult" abstraction would be activated across cats, dogs, and other animals.

Being presented with the words Puppy and Dog would then retrieve this abstraction of "adult" that exists across animals. If they are then presented with the next part of the analogy, Kitten, the abstraction of "adult" would still be active in their brain. Being presented with Kitten and "adult" would now lead to Cat being recalled through pattern completion. Again, this is the correct answer to the analogy.

However, what if the abstraction is not perceived or understood? Then, there would not be a common element between Puppy and Dog, and Kitten and Cat. So Puppy and Dog would not activate an element that is also associated with Kitten and Cat. So being presented with Puppy and Dog followed by Kitten would be similar to being presented with the word Kitten alone and being asked what the answer is. Kitten by itself would not retrieve Cat by pattern completion, so someone who does not understand the abstraction would not be able to retrieve or know the correct answer. They would be just as likely to say Hamster as this is another small pet they may have had.

Finally, we have Number Series. Again, we can see how abstraction and pattern completion are central to solving these problems. For the first number series problem, the numbers were 2, 4, 6, and 8. Abstraction leads to the knowledge that there is commonality across these numbers, namely that the gap is the same from one number to the next. Pattern completion would then repeat this pattern of 2, 2, 2 to the final number of 8, leading to the answer of 10. Even the most complex number series problems involve seeing the abstract patterns present in the series, and then repeating this pattern to determine the correct answer.

These examples demonstrate that an auto-associative network coupled with a cerebral cortex that learns abstractions can be very useful. It can not only learn information quickly, but can also generalize this information across many different situations based on consistencies present within the environment. Or, putting it in a more technical way, it can respond rapidly to changing circumstances while at the same time honoring the structure of the environment that is stable and leads to predictability across situations.

SAVANT SYNDROME

Let us now consider savant syndrome.[146] The case of savants are frequently raised when extreme intellectual performance and even genius are discussed. However, savants are individuals who measure low in IQ. This low IQ may even mean that they have difficulty living independently and caring for themselves.

Despite this, they also exhibit striking performance in one or more domains. In arithmetic, they may be able to quickly multiply two extremely large numbers together without needing to write down any steps to determine the solution. A savant who is good at prime numbers can identify whether or not an extremely large number such as

134,950,801 is a prime number (incidentally, it is). Savants who are good at date calculation can identify what day any particular date falls on. Drawing involves being able to look at a scene once and then creating an incredibly detailed illustration of the scene. Music involves being able to listen to a musical performance only once and then being able to repeat it accurately.

Not only is a savant's performance in these domains much greater than would be expected based on their IQ, but their performance can even be well beyond that of people with extremely high IQs. How can we account for these performances?

The Effect of Practice

We can begin by observing that the performance of savants is, perhaps, not as exceptional as it appears. It may seem amazing that someone would know whether the number 134,950,801 is a prime number or not. However, a typical person also has little interest in whether particular large numbers are prime numbers or not. On the other hand, savants are different. They become obsessed with the domain in which they eventually show amazing performance. They may spend hours a day practicing the multiplication of numbers, or examining whether numbers are primes. And we all know that performance improves with practice.

Despite this, people will often claim that they cannot believe that they could become so good at these tasks—even with thousands of hours of practice. However, psychological studies have shown that college students can attain levels of performance beyond the range of normal adult performance following just a few weeks of practice or training on tasks such as mental arithmetic and date calculation.[147] Savants also tend to be isolated from the world and not be occupied by the activities that most people engage in. This gives them much more time to practice these skills and become remarkable experts.

Lack of Abstraction

However, using the above framework, we can make another observation. The performances of savants tend to be performances that do not involve abstraction, but rather rote memorization of an extreme number of concrete instances. Therefore, it is perhaps not an accident that these performances tend to be given by people with lower IQs. Their lack of abstraction means that their auto-associative networks are more able to learn patterns based on lower-level inputs, such as elementary numbers.

Consider the example of drawing. A savant may look at a scene of a city once and draw it in fine detail. A more typical person will not notice many of these details, and so will not be able to draw them.

However, this is not the only difference. The savant may be able to draw the scene of the city in fine detail, but they will also have a poor understanding of what they are seeing. They will not be able to anticipate when is the best time to cross the street without being hit by a car, or understand that the gutters on the street are designed to channel the water and also prevent cars from mounting the sidewalk.

On the other hand, the inability of a typical person to notice many details of a scene is adaptive. Many fine details of a scene have no relevance for that person's interaction with the environment. Consequently, their brain has learned to filter out these details. Instead, they notice features of the environment that determine its predictability. This enables them to interact with the environment more effectively.

Consistent with this, while savant performance is often considered to be remarkable, it is typically not considered to show the inventive or

145

novel characteristics of true genius. In other words, such performances tend to be more mechanical in their reproduction, rather than representing true insight and understanding. Studies have observed this.[148]

HOW DIGITAL COMPUTERS ARE DIFFERENT

We also talked briefly in Chapter One about how difficult it has been to get digital computers to identify even the simplest abstractions. This does not mean that digital computers are necessarily inferior to humans when it comes to processing information. These days, even home computers can perform millions of calculations per second. They can use this computational power to perform calculations such as simulating the flow of air across an aircraft's wings, applying advanced statistical formulas thousands of times, and simulating neural networks in the brain. These calculations were simply not possible before the advent of computers. It would take a person literally thousands of years to perform these types of computations. So, digital computers are clearly superior to humans at some tasks.

There are also some tasks that humans and digital computers are both good at. One example is playing chess. Supercomputers have been created that can defeat the best human chess players in the world. Given that chess has been considered to be a game that requires great intelligence for humans to play successfully, this has led to the conclusion by some that digital computers are now equal to humans in intelligence.

However, this is not true. While digital computers can play chess very well, they play chess in a different way to humans.[149] Humans think very slowly—it can take seconds for a person to understand a situation and formulate a response. On the other hand, as we have already observed, digital computers can perform millions of calculations in the same time. Digital computers can also be very systematic in these calculations, as long as they are programmed correctly.

This means that a computer can be programmed to play chess not by "knowing" the correct response to make based on past experience, but by simply evaluating all of the possible combinations of moves that could be made next. It can then choose the move that will have the most favorable outcome. It is a brute-force method of trying all available options, rather than "understanding" the situation and using this understanding to determine the best course of action. As computers have become faster, this brute-force method has proven superior to human intelligence in situations such as chess.

However, in other situations such as perception, a brute-force approach is not suitable. Chess is a relatively constrained environment in which only certain moves are permissible, and the chess board limits the number of options. This makes a brute-force approach feasible. In perception, the number of combinations can quickly become astronomical. Consider the number of different objects that you could be presented with and asked to identify. Now think of combinations of those objects.

More importantly, chess is a situation where the opponent's options are also limited, and the goal is rigidly defined. This enables an opponent's responses to be predicted and evaluated. In the real world, the responses of other people and the environment are not so predictable. This means that it is not possible to simulate all possible combinations of events and assess the appropriate outcome. For example, consider speech recognition. How can a computer correctly determine a command that is given to it by simulating its response to every possible command that may be made by a human, and then determining whether it is what the human wanted or not?

In these situations, the failures of computers have been quite evident, despite the numerous promises of computer researchers for decades. Even the most advanced computers are unable to display perception skills that are equal to those of a five-year-old child. This lack of success highlights the fact that the digital computer and the human brain are quite different in the way they process information.

Transistors and Wires versus Neurons and Connections

Why are computers different? Digital computers differ in that they are based on transistors rather than neurons. Unlike neurons, transistors *are* switches.[150] This allows information to be arbitrarily directed through the computer, like the train network analogy we gave in Chapter Four. Because of this ability to reroute information through a computer, a given piece of information can be stored at any location in a computer's memory. On the other hand, in the human brain, the meaning of activity in a neuron depends on which other neurons it is connected to. In other words, the location of a memory determines what the memory is.

However, perhaps even more importantly, the human brain has the ability to change its connections in response to experience. This process is what enables abstraction to be learned over time in the human brain. On the other hand, the wires in digital computers are permanently etched into crystallized silicon.

Consider the implications of this for speech recognition, a task that we have already talked about. Recognizing speech is based on recognizing phonemes. Phonemes are the individual sounds that make up the words in our spoken language. For instance, both "cat" and "kit" start with the /k/ sound or phoneme. Recognizing different phonemes is an example of abstraction, and high-IQ children learn speech recognition earlier.

When you hear the /k/ sound, the receptors in your ear will receive information that indicates the presence of the phoneme. However, your ear receives a lot of other information that is not necessarily related to the presence of the /k/ sound. There will be information that will differ based on whether the speaker is a male or a female. There will also be information that will indicate what area they grew up in. Further, there will be information that is unique to the individual who is speaking.

As we saw in Chapter Four, the neural connections in the brain adapt over childhood so that they ignore information that varies from one concrete instance to the next. Only information that is in common across the concrete instances is retained. In this case, the information in common is the information that occurs when different people make the same /k/ sound.[151]

As has already been noted, often we do not even know how we perceive these sounds ourselves. What characteristics of a sound define the presence of the /k/ phoneme? What distinguishes the /k/ sound from the /d/ phoneme in dog? If you hear either of these phonemes, you can immediately identify them correctly. However, you typically do not consciously know what in the sound allows you to discriminate between them—it just seems obvious.[152] You are able to identify them because *exposure* to them during childhood changed your neural connections, allowing your brain to automatically perceive them.[153]

On the other hand, consider the problem from the digital computer's perspective. It can have a microphone that provides it with the same auditory information that we receive from our ears. However, this

149

information includes not only information about the presence of the phoneme, but also information about the speaker's gender, their background, and unique characteristics of their voice. All of this information is processed and stored. If the same person repeats the same sound, the computer can then compare the two sounds and confirm that they are the same phoneme (assuming a lack of background noise).

However, if someone else speaks, much of this sound information will be different—irrespective of whether the person has spoken the same phoneme or not. Digital computers do not go through a learning process whereby their wires change so that irrelevant information is filtered out. Computers take everything in an exact and literal sense, so both the relevant and irrelevant information are still present in the computer's representation of the sound.

This detailed representation is what makes it difficult for a computer to compare the sound with a previously-heard sound and determine whether it is the same phoneme or not. All of the other information gets in the way, distracting the computer from seeing the commonality across the situations. This means that the process of abstraction that we take for granted is something that computers, in their present form with fixed wiring, will always find difficult.[154]

It may also be argued that computers do not possess understanding, but are simply following a set of instructions or a program that was written by a human who did "understand" the task that needed to be performed. To a computer, it is only manipulating symbols based on rigidly defined rules. These rules were designed by humans so that they could anticipate the outcome of the computer's processing. They then use this anticipation of the outcome to define the instructions required to get the outcome that is needed. In other words, the human programmer is serving as the homunculus that is telling the computer *which* switches should be changed and *when*.

Turing Machines

Advocates of using digital computers to understand human intelligence and produce artificial intelligence will also sometimes argue that both digital computers and the human brain can be considered to be "Turing machines." This term came from the work of Alan Turing, who showed that there is a set of fundamental operations. A machine that can perform these operations can solve any computational function.[155] In this view, even though digital computers are different in construction to the human brain, it makes no difference to their computational ability.

However, what this argument fails to take into account is a sense of efficiency and scale. Humans can solve any computational function, but we can be very slow at doing it. Consider a human manually calculating a very large spreadsheet. None of the spreadsheet calculations are operations that a human could not perform, so a human could calculate exactly the same result as a computer. However, computers can do these calculations millions of times faster. This is why computers have revolutionized many different fields.

Still, the same argument also applies in reverse. It is possible to program a digital computer to simulate the neurons in a human brain. There is nothing magical about these neurons. Their properties may be reduced down to electrophysiological properties and mathematical equations that describe what occurs physically in the brain.[156]

Yet, this does not mean that digital computers can easily produce the same results as the human brain. Again because of scale and efficiency.

While the human brain is slow at doing universal computational functions, it is specialized, as a result of evolution, to have the capacity to identify abstractions. It does this using billions of neurons and trillions of neural connections.

On the other hand, scientists simulating the brain can require a supercomputer to accurately recreate the function of just a single neuron. To overcome this problem, many simplifying assumptions of neuron behavior can be made. This enables scientists to simulate groups or networks of neurons. However, there is a limit to how much simplification can be carried out. And even with simplifications, a large network of neurons can still be beyond the simulation capacity of even the fastest current computers, especially when the simulation is required to be in real time for many applications such that the simulated neurons must process information as quickly as real neurons. In other words, how useful is it for a digital computer to successfully recognize a spoken word if it takes three weeks of processing to do so?

While the computational power of digital computers has increased massively over the last few decades, there will always be limits as to how efficiently a digital computer can simulate neurons when the underlying architectures are so different. This suggests that the current digital computer paradigm may always find artificial intelligence to be a challenge. Instead, the design of computers needs to take into account how the brain works if they are to be successful in this area.

Consciousness and Understanding

We have so far learned how the brain is able to change its neural connections over childhood, and how this process corresponds to the increasing ability to understand abstractions. However, we have not yet explained what this book set out to do at the beginning—namely, explain what it actually means to *understand.*

This is a difficult question to answer. When we "understand" something, we can perceive it or see it in our mind. This entails the notion of *consciousness.* In other words, when we perceive something, we are aware or conscious of it. So, understanding "understanding" is ultimately a question about what consciousness is.[157]

However, many readers will be aware that this is entangling us in a philosophical issue that has been debated for many centuries.[158] What is consciousness? Is it a product of the human brain? If so, how does the human brain create it?

We saw in Chapter Four that different areas of the cerebral cortex are responsible for thinking about different things. This means that damage to these areas can result in people not being "aware" or conscious of what is normally processed in those areas. For instance, it is found that damage to a particular region of the cortical area responsible for processing visual information can result in a complete loss of color vision, while the ability to discriminate differences in shading is unimpaired. Strikingly, it is found that people with these lesions cannot even imagine colors or remember the colors of objects that they saw before their brain suffered the lesion.[159]

These findings suggest that consciousness is not due to neurons firing in a special "part" of the brain. Damage to a specific part of the cerebral cortex results in an impairment to a specific aspect of conscious experience. What seems to be a unitary sense of consciousness is actually distributed throughout the cortex, with different regions being important for our ability to be aware or conscious of different features in our environment.

However, identifying how the cerebral cortex produces consciousness is more challenging. A simple view would argue that whatever neurons are firing in the cerebral cortex determines what we are conscious of. However, this simple approach does not work. It is found that neurons are continually active and firing in the brain—whether we are conscious of what they represent or not. Neurons also fire very rapidly, 50 times per second on average.[160] However, our thoughts do not change 50 times each second—it tends to take us around a full second to move from one thought to the next.[161] This suggests that the answer to how the brain produces consciousness is more complex than simply which neurons are firing in the brain at a given time.

Donald Hebb and Neural Assemblies

To provide an answer to the problem of consciousness, we are going to borrow from the work of Donald Hebb.[162] Hebb noted that the cerebral cortex is also distinctive in that it has many feedback connections. By feedback connections, we mean connections that go back from one cortical region to another. Far from neural activation being a one-way process from the senses up through the brain to the muscles, the cerebral cortex is just as likely to send information in the reverse direction as well.

Hebb argued that the feed-forward and feedback connections, or two-way communication between different areas of the cerebral cortex, would result in what he described as *neural assemblies*. Neural assemblies were said to occur when neurons fired back and forth between each other and became synchronized in their firing.

This synchronization of neural firings was then argued to be the underlying basis of what we are conscious of. While neurons in the cerebral cortex are always active, only those that are currently synchronized with each other represent what we are currently "aware" of.

This account fits with how quickly we "think." While neurons are always firing in the brain, it takes a set of neurons a while to settle into a neural assembly and to synchronize their firing. Only once this has happened are we "conscious" of what the synchronization is representing. Essentially, the synchronization is saying that while there is a lot of activity going on in the brain, let us pull out some specific activity and amplify it via the feedback connections. We then become more aware of it as these firings are reinforced or become more active, while other neural firings in the brain are not being reinforced—they are more akin to background noise.

This notion of feedback being related to consciousness has been supported by fMRI studies.[163] When someone is asked to imagine a visual stimulus such as a painting, the cortical area normally responsible for receiving visual input becomes active—as if they really are seeing the visual stimulus. On the other hand, if they are asked to play back a song in their mind, the cortical area that would normally be active when they are listening to the song becomes active. This indicates that the feedback connections are able to stimulate the early sensory cortical areas and effectively recreate the input that occurred when the stimulus was experienced for real.

You can also see this effect for yourself. If you are near a window, look at the window. Then think about the shape of the window. When you think of the abstraction "square" or "rectangle," the shape of the window seems to jump out, while other features of the environment seem to retreat or are no longer as noticeable. Indeed, even if there is something obscuring part of the window, we can still see the complete square that makes up the window. This reflects the activation of lower cortical areas by higher areas, and allows us to recognize and extract out salient features of the environment from the current context. Various other scientific studies have also supported the belief that synchronization of neural firings across the cortex is responsible for the sense of awareness or consciousness that we experience.[164]

Understanding "Understanding"

Let us now think about what this synchronization really means for "understanding." When we understand something, we are saying that the brain has been able to form a neural assembly or feedback loop such that activation leading up the brain is greeted by the same activation coming back down again. What does this mean?

At the neural level, the stimulation the brain is getting *corresponds* to the stimulation it expects based on past experience. In other words, it *understands* it. This is not just a play on words. Saying that you understand something means that what occurred is what you would expect to occur. The formation of a neural assembly or a sense of understanding represents this process at the neural level. What happened is what your brain *expected* to happen based on past experience!

Once again, this emphasizes the importance of childhood experience and changing the neural connections. In order to perceive an abstraction, the brain must be able to form a neural assembly that binds its elements together. However, as described in Chapter Four, neurons are not switches. In other words, activation cannot be arbitrarily routed around the brain based on what is being perceived. So, any required neural assembly cannot be formed just by throwing a few switches and getting neural activity to go the right way.

Instead, in order for a neural assembly or synchronization to form, the correct connections need to be present. If the correct connections are present, a neural assembly can occur when a person is presented with a concrete instance of the given abstraction. This leads to the perception of the abstraction, or an understanding of the situation. On the other hand, if the appropriate connections are not present, the brain will not be able to form a neural assembly when it is presented with the abstraction. The person will not get the sense of consciousness that allows them to say that they "see" or "understand" it.

So, understanding depends on how the brain is connected. When we perceive an abstraction, we do so at the time we are presented with it. However, what enables us to perceive it at this time is childhood experience of the abstraction that changed the connections in our brain. This experience enables the brain to recognize and represent the abstraction in later life. On the other hand, if children do not get this experience, they will not have the appropriate connections that allow the abstraction to be represented in their brain when they are exposed to the abstraction later on. Once again, this suggests that childhood experience is *critical*.

CHAPTER SEVEN

A SENSITIVE PERIOD FOR LEARNING THE ABILITY TO UNDERSTAND

Both brain science and child psychology tell us that the developing brain differs from the adult brain. We have also learned that the ability to understand abstractions increases in childhood but not adulthood. Indeed, the ability to understand abstractions is greatest in young adulthood.

Nonetheless, when we think of the adult brain, it is tempting to think that it has a homunculus in it that is especially good at understanding abstractions. No matter what the abstraction is, the homunculus or little person in the brain can reroute the neural activity and lead to an understanding of the abstraction.

However, as we have seen, this homunculus explanation of human intelligence is not satisfactory. The brain does not have a homunculus that is able to reroute neural activity at the time that thoughts are occurring. Instead, activity is rerouted through the brain as a consequence of gradually changing the connections over childhood. This learning process leads to the increasing ability to understand abstractions.

Since the ability to understand abstractions improves over childhood but not adulthood, this indicates that the learning process responsible for learning abstractions is active in the developing brain and not the adult brain. This is supported by brain science showing that the pruning of the neural connections is a process that occurs specifically during childhood, and that the growth cones that direct this pruning process are not found in the adult brain. Hence, the developing brain is more able to adapt its neural connections based on experience.

This leads to perhaps the most important implication of this book—that there is a sensitive period for learning understanding. By sensitive period, we mean that there is a certain age range during which experience is most effective. If we say that there is a sensitive period up until sixteen years of age, this indicates that receiving intellectual stimulation during this time can lead to changes in the neural connections and a consequent change in the ability to understand. If adults receive the equivalent experience, this does not lead to the same improvement in the ability to understand the underlying abstraction.

The concept of sensitive periods for development is ubiquitous in the brain sciences.[165] This evidence has come from the experimental freedom to control when animals are provided with a certain experience. As we have seen, even perceiving something as simple as horizontal or vertical lines will depend on environmental stimulation during a sensitive period. If the perception of lines depends on a sensitive period, it seems reasonable to suggest that perceiving more complex patterns in our environment also depends on learning during a sensitive period. However, is there direct evidence that adults have greater difficulty than children in learning to understand abstractions?

Direct Evidence for a Sensitive Period

There are many domains that we could investigate. We will focus on the core domains of language, literacy, and mathematics.

Language

There are many parallels between language and abstraction. Not only do words often represent abstractions, but our ability to understand a novel sentence is like our ability to solve an abstraction problem. In both cases, we are presented with a combination of elements that is new. If our ability to understand was based just on our exact memory of past concrete instances, we would be unable to either understand the novel sentence or solve the abstraction problem.

Instead, both language and abstraction problems involve taking abstract principles that we already understand and rearranging them into novel combinations. This commonality is supported by the observation that more-intelligent children often display superior language skills. The speed with which a child acquires language is also an indicator of their giftedness.[166]

There is also evidence that language only develops because children are given the appropriate stimulation when they are young. We have already mentioned cases of extreme deprivation such as The Wild Boy of Aveyron and Genie.[167] These children were brought up without a normal language environment. Consequently, when they were discovered by authorities, their language abilities were greatly impaired. Considerable effort was then made to teach these children in adulthood the language skills that normal children learn during childhood. Unfortunately, these interventions—ultimately much more intensive than those a typical child would ever receive—failed to result in normal language function being acquired. These individuals did develop the ability to understand simple words, but they were never able to form complete grammatically correct sentences or express complex ideas through language.

These examples may not be all that convincing, as these children may already have suffered from intellectual impairments. However, these cases certainly do not provide evidence that learning language in adulthood, when the ability to understand is supposed to be at a maximum, is easy.

What about children who are given a normal, nurturing environment while they are growing up? In fact, it is easy to find evidence that adults are less able to learn languages. Someone born in a particular country is likely to develop language skills that identify them as a "native speaker" of the language of that country. The term "native speaker" recognizes that people who are not born into a particular language environment are likely to find it more difficult to learn the language. Indeed, everyone knows people who have moved to another country in adulthood where a different language is spoken. If they never spoke the new language in childhood, their language abilities are likely to always identify them as not having been born in the new country.

This intuitive observation has also been supported by psychological research. For instance, Jacqueline Johnson and Elissa Newport investigated second-language acquisition of Chinese and Korean migrants to America.[168] The migrants were controlled for the number of years of exposure to English, but differed in age of initial exposure. It was found that ultimate language proficiency in grammar was a direct function of the age of initial exposure. The younger the person was, the higher the level of proficiency obtained. However, this relationship only held until sixteen years of age. After this age, age of arrival had no further impact on ultimate grammar attainment. Many other language researchers also support the view that there is a sensitive period for language acquisition.[169]

It is also often said that children learn languages differently than adults.[170] Children learn to speak a language fluently without being told which words are adjectives, adverbs, etc. They learn language just by exposure to the language alone. Again, this is consistent with the learning process that was described in Chapter Four, whereby a child learns the structure of experience simply through exposure to concrete instances of that structure.

Adults, on the other hand, do not learn this way. They need to be taught explicitly the words and principles of grammar that make up a language. Their learning of a language is more consistent with crystallized knowledge, whereby associations between new words and meanings are learned through an auto-associative network based on their current ability to understand.

Literacy

What about literacy? Reading would seem to be a simple task. You look at a page of text, immediately perceiving the words that are written there. For this reason, many people assume that there is not a sensitive period for learning to read. How could someone have difficulty learning something that seems so easy?

However, people who believe this forget their childhood. When they were a young child, they did not have the ability to look at a page and immediately perceive the individual letters and words independent of the context. They learned this ability by spending many years in school learning to read. While they may have forgotten many of the details of their schooling, this reading experience has remained with them. It *changed* their neural connections. Words are able to be perceived because the connections have learned to filter out information that is irrelevant to the perception of the word, such as font type, size, and color. Words may then be perceived across different contexts, even when many of these details change. It is this change in the neural connections over childhood that allows adults to "immediately" perceive the word and makes it seem so "simple."

Literacy is also an early indicator of intelligence, suggesting that, again, there is commonality between identifying words in different contexts and identifying abstractions in different situations.

So, if reading is due to the same process that is responsible for learning other abstractions, there should also be a sensitive period for learning to read. In fact, there is evidence to suggest that this is the case.

Cecil Smith and Thomas Reio were strong advocates for adult literacy programs, and undertook a study intending to portray the programs in a favorable light. However, what they found was very different. They found that adult literacy programs made no statistically significant difference to adult literacy compared with controls who did not participate in the programs. In other words, adult literacy programs did not improve literacy skills![171]

This is likely to upset some people, who will argue that we should not say that adults are limited in what they can and cannot learn. However, saying that adults can acquire literacy in adulthood will not suddenly change biology and make it easy for adults to acquire literacy if literacy depends on brain mechanisms that are more active in childhood. In addition, when an adult has difficulties learning to read, this must have a negative impact on their self-esteem—especially when they see so many children master with seeming ease what they are finding so challenging.

On the other hand, being candid about human abilities has benefits. Imagine an adult who did not receive appropriate experience in childhood for literacy skills. Providing information about the sensitive period will at least explain why they are finding it so difficult to learn literacy in adulthood. It will tell them that their difficulties are not due to some innate deficiency in their intelligence but a lack of opportunity. Also, if they do succeed in improving their literacy skills, they will rightly feel that it is a great accomplishment.

However, the consequences go beyond this. The reality is that children who are most at risk of not learning to read and write are children of parents who lack literacy skills. These parents won't be able to teach their children themselves, and are likely to view reading and writing as being too challenging. After all, if they as adults are finding it so difficult, then what chance is there for their children to master literacy—especially when in other respects the parents know that they have a greater ability to understand than their children do? These parents are less likely to make sure that their children receive appropriate stimulation to develop literacy skills. They are more likely to accept poor performance in literacy, as they know that they themselves cannot do any better. This is likely to perpetuate a lack of reading skills that is passed on from one generation to the next.

On the other hand, what if it is acknowledged that there is a sensitive period? Then, these parents will know that their difficulties stem not from some innate limitation, but from missing out on reading and writing experience during childhood. They will then view it as essential that their children get this experience that they missed out on. They will believe that their children can acquire literacy skills even though they themselves find it so challenging. This will ultimately lead to better educational outcomes.

Mathematics

Another obvious example is mathematics. Again, mathematics is like the abstraction problems we have already discussed. To solve a mathematical problem, you need to apply abstractions in a novel situation to determine the correct answer.

However, any college professor who teaches mathematics to students without a mathematical background knows just how difficult many adults find mathematics. It is by no means the case that adults—with their mature level of understanding—will suddenly find it easy to learn mathematical concepts that they found difficult in their youth. Indeed, college degrees with a mathematical component will often get around this problem by making it mandatory for students taking the course to have already studied mathematics to a required level in school. Further, mathematics in college does not consist of understanding new abstractions. Rather, students are taught new procedures using principles or abstractions that they already learned in childhood.

Compared with literacy, there has been even less work done examining the effectiveness of adult mathematics programs. However, what little work has been done has again noted the lack of effectiveness of adult programs that teach basic mathematics.[172]

The Role of School

This then raises the question of why we send children to school. An initial answer might be that school teaches children a lot of facts or knowledge. However, does this really make sense? Can you name all of your school teachers? Can you name *any* of your school teachers? These are people who came into your classroom and addressed you every day for a whole year. However, it is not only teachers' names that you likely cannot remember. Can you remember what subjects you covered in school? What about the specific topics that were taught in those subjects? It is actually quite common to find that adults are unable to remember not only what they were taught in school, but even that they were taught the subject at all!

This really calls into question the point of sending children to school for so many years in childhood. Children would be happier if they were given the freedom to play with friends and have fun, rather than sitting in a classroom for hours each day. If children forget most of what they learn in school, what purpose does it serve to teach them this information in the first place?

In addition, one of the striking characteristics of college is just how much more capable adults are at learning new information. In a typical college course with just 25 hours of lecture time, it is not uncommon to cover more material than is covered in a similar subject in a whole year in high school. The amount of information covered in primary school is less again! If you go back and look at your old school syllabus, you will find that months were spent teaching you information that only takes you a few moments to learn now.

So if adults are so much better at learning facts and knowledge than children, why not wait until maturity before trying to teach people? If

167

the ability to understand abstractions developed through some innate or genetic program, then it would develop whether children went to school or not. If you waited until adulthood, then children who were having difficulty understanding their schoolwork would be more likely to be able to understand the material as their abilities would have had longer to mature. This would give them greater confidence in their abilities.

Clearly, there is something wrong this interpretation. It comes from not appreciating the real value of school.

The True Importance of School

The importance of school is not in the facts or knowledge taught to children. As has been pointed out, most of us will forget most if not all of this information by the time we reach adulthood. What school is important for is teaching children the ability to understand abstractions. The slow speed of instruction and the many, many concrete examples of abstractions children get at school gives their brains the required information to prune their connections in such a way that they can perceive abstractions independent of the context that accompanies the general principles. Once this pruning process has occurred, children can then recognize the abstractions—not only in the context of the concrete instances that they were taught, but in other situations as well.

School does this so well that adults can completely forget the massive amount of time and effort that it took them in childhood to be able to understand abstractions that they take for granted as adults. Since school changes the neural connections so that abstractions are more easily recognized, perceiving abstractions can seem to be automatic and effortless. The abstraction can seem so obvious that it just seems a natural outcome of being presented with a concrete example of the abstraction. It can be difficult to appreciate that it is something that needed to be learned originally.

You might not have seen an abstraction for years since being taught it in school. However, in contrast to memory for facts that you tend to forget, you will still immediately perceive the abstraction the next time you see it without needing to think about it—like how fractions can be used to divide up an amount, or how a graph represents information. This is because the changes in the neural connections that lead to the perception of abstractions are much more permanent than the changes that occur for memory.

HOW COLLEGE DIFFERS

Once children reach adulthood, they then move on to college. College is very different from school in the way children are taught. As we have already mentioned, college covers much more material in a given amount of time than school does. It is able to do this because professors do not need to worry about teaching abstractions to their students. Instead, college consists of teaching students configurations and sequences of abstractions that they already understand.

For instance, in high school, students are taught the basic principles of algebra. At college, students are shown how to apply these principles to sets of numbers in grids known as matrices. They are then shown how to apply this matrix mathematics in many different applications, including physics, chemistry, and statistics. Indeed, complex mathematical models of neural networks in the brain are built on matrices that are ultimately based on the simple algebraic abstractions taught at school. More generally, people are able to understand college material because it involves the same abstractions as school work. Because the students are already able to understand the abstractions, the material may be covered much faster. Often, the material is explained only once, in contrast to the numerous examples and exercises that are characteristic of school.

This difference in teaching at school versus college is also highlighted by how learning is assessed. At school, at the start of the year, the goal may be to ensure that children have reached mastery of a concept by the end of the school year. Assessment will then be made at the end of the year to confirm that they understand the concept. There is such a long time between the start of instruction and assessment because it is recognized that it will take a lot of instruction and a long period of time for children to develop a genuine understanding of the abstraction. This is consistent with learning that is dependent on physically changing the neural connections—a slow process that can take months or even longer to occur.

Contrast this with the way assessment works at college. Individual courses may be as short as six weeks. Final assessment of material can occur within a few days of its *first* presentation to students! This time frame is much too short for the neural connections to physically change in response to environmental stimulation, like they do during childhood. Instead, the only way that students can understand the material in such a short time is if their neural connections are already in the right configuration. Having their neural connections in the right configuration from childhood experience will enable them to understand the abstraction when it is presented to them in later life, such as in college.

Darwin at College

We have learned that psychological tests indicate that the ability to understand abstractions does not increase in adulthood like childhood. However, some readers might be questioning whether this is really true. Does not the complexity of material at college show that adults are still able to learn to understand new abstractions, contradicting the psychological findings? How are college students able to pass all of their courses and graduate if they are unable to increase their ability to understand?

However, believing that college is about increasing the ability to understand abstractions is fundamentally misunderstanding the nature of college education. Unlike school, where the goal is to have every child succeed, college is based more on Darwin's principle of survival of the fittest. More students are admitted to a college degree than there are jobs available at the end of the degree. Those who pass all of their courses and graduate are the students who possess the ability to understand the course material. Those who do not have the ability to understand the material will fail their courses and not complete their degree.

Indeed, colleges are often very unforgiving toward students who show difficulty understanding the material. Often, students who fail a subject will only be given one further chance to successfully pass the subject. If they do not pass the subject on their second attempt, they will be prevented from enrolling in that subject again.

This is the opposite of what you would expect if understanding developed in adulthood over the course of months or even years through experience. If it did, then you would expect that there would be subjects where many students would *fail* the first time, given how short college courses are. However, they would be given the opportunity to retake and retake the course until they eventually learned to understand the material. Since college does not work this way, it again tells us that adult learning is different to child learning.

LATER ADULT LIFE

What about later life? Is there evidence that older adults can increase their ability to understand?

Professors

Let us consider the example of professors at college. Professors have a very intellectually stimulating life, continually investigating new topics and forming new conclusions. However, this does not necessarily mean that their actual ability to understand abstractions increases over this time. We will see in the next chapter how major scientific advances are typically made by young researchers—those who have much less experience but whose ability to understand is shown by psychological tests to be at a maximum.

Instead of professors typically learning to understand new abstractions, their work involves finding out which particular abstractions that they already understand are required to explain particular scientific questions. This is illustrated by the success of scientific conferences, where professors present their research to other professors. Typically, a professor has been studying a highly specialized domain for many years. If the professor has learned new abstractions over the years in which he or she has been studying the domain, how would other professors in the audience be able to understand the professor's presentation when they typically have been studying *other* very specialized domains? The presentation should be beyond their understanding, and they would need to study the particular domain for years if they are to understand what the other professor is talking about.

Instead, a professor is able to understand the presentations of other professors at a conference even though their interests may be quite different. The reason that they are able to understand other professors' talks is because they have the ability to understand the majority of the abstractions that are used in the field.

How is it that they are able to understand the majority of the abstractions that are used in the field? Again, the explanation lies with Darwin and the principle of natural selection. Becoming a professor is very competitive. First, you need to get a PhD, which is obtained by demonstrating the ability to do successful independent research in the field. However, entrance to the PhD program itself is extremely competitive, and is determined by grades in college. Since entrance to PhD programs is so competitive, it is typically the students with the best grades who are admitted to the PhD programs.

How do students get the best grades? By being very good at understanding the abstractions used in the field! If a student has the top grades in a course over a number of years, this confirms that they are very able to understand the abstractions required to understand the field. They will then be given the opportunity to eventually become a professor.[173]

The reason that this culling process and survival of the fittest principle works is because students entering a degree program will differ in their ability to understand the material. Professors will often quickly get a sense of the "good" students in the course—the ones that have the potential to go on to a PhD. These will be the "A" students. Professors will know the "A" students because they will typically construct exams such that in order to get an "A," you really need to *understand* the material.

They assess understanding by requiring students to apply the information they have been taught to new contexts. The students who are good at understanding will be able to do this.

On the other hand, there will be other students who are not "A" students. These students often work just as hard as the "A" students, but they find the material difficult to understand. They do well on exam questions that involve rote memorization, but they struggle when exam questions involve applying the material to new contexts. These students are not given the opportunity to move on to a PhD and become a professor in the field because their grades will be too low—reflecting their difficulty in understanding the relevant abstractions. So, the ability to understand is not something that is developed while you are a professor. It is identified well beforehand.

In the Workplace

This variation in understanding is evident in the workplace as well. Some jobs are relatively easy, such that rote memorization is sufficient for highly efficient performance. However, there are other jobs that require flexibility. To do well in these jobs requires the understanding of abstractions.

Employers recognize this. They will look at a graduate's grades to determine whether they are a good candidate or not. While the job may require little knowledge that was actually taught in the degree, they know that a graduate who struggled to pass their courses is less likely to understand the abstractions required to be successful on the job—even if the occupation involves extensive on-the-job training.

What happens if someone who has difficulty understanding the required abstractions is still given the job? Everyone knows of someone who has been in their job for 10 years or more, but they are still not "good" at their work. They will be slow to produce results, and will often make excuses for not getting the work done. They rely on trial and error, or someone with a better understanding to continually help them out. Meanwhile, a new recruit can arrive and almost immediately start displaying better performance. Even though they have only been in the job for a short time, they understand the required abstractions, as opposed to the long-time employee.

Adults will often deal with difficulties in understanding abstractions by simply memorizing concrete instances of the abstractions, and admit that they do not really understand them. This can also lead to self selection in terms of narrowing career options. People will often recognize that they are not "cut out" for a particular task or domain, and will change their interests to another task or domain that they find easier to understand.

While this may sound pessimistic, the crucial point is that understanding abstractions is not something that is easy and can be taken for granted. Rather, understanding is a challenge, and it needs to be recognized as such. Further, it depends on a learning process that psychological evidence and brain science suggest is more active in childhood.

WHY WOULD THERE BE A SENSITIVE PERIOD?

Given the usefulness of being able to understand, this begs the question of *why* there might be a sensitive period for learning to understand. It would seem better if the ability to understand continued to increase throughout life—not just during childhood but during adulthood as well. However, there are several possible reasons to explain a sensitive period for learning the ability to understand.

Humans Are Not Perfect

While it may be advantageous for the ability to understand to increase in adulthood like it does in childhood, this does not mean that it would necessarily be true. Arguing this is saying that just because something would be better for humans to possess, then evolution would have resulted in humans possessing it. However, there are numerous examples where evolution does not result in the most efficient or effective outcome.

One example is DNA itself. It is known that there is a lot of genetic material that does not seem to serve any function in DNA. This material, described as junk DNA, continues to be reproduced and carried from one generation to the next. This is because the costs of carrying it are relatively small and do not determine survival outcomes.

Another example of inefficiency is the eye. The receptors of the eye are located *behind* the nerve fibers that carry information out of the eye. This means that light needs to go through these nerve fibers to reach the receptors. This reduces the information that is made available to the receptors, and leads to poorer acuity. And yet, evolution has not led to a more efficient or effective outcome.

Similarly, the brain itself is inefficient. Transmission at the neural connections is based on the diffusion of chemicals from one neuron to the next. This results in neural transmission being a very slow process, reducing our speed of response to dangerous situations in the environment. Also, at least some of the complexity in the brain is unlikely to be necessary, but is due to imperfections that achieve a given function using many more neurons than are required.

These examples are not surprising, as the theory of evolution does not argue that an organism needs to be perfectly efficient to survive.

All that is required is a selective advantage relative to other organisms with which it is competing. So, even though our ability to understand only increases in childhood, the human species still has a substantial advantage over other animals that do not develop this same ability to understand. It may be that the ability to understand will increase in adulthood in future generations. However, this capability has not yet evolved because the human species is not yet at the end point of evolution.

Developing Understanding is Based on a Developmental Process

We have seen how a pruning mechanism allows the extraction of general principles by filtering out information that is irrelevant to those general principles. It appears as though this process originated as a mechanism for the nervous system to form connections during its initial development. This suggests that humans are not limited by this process only occurring until maturity. Rather, humans are benefited by this process having been extended over a longer period of time compared with other animals. In this way, our brains have become more adaptable to the environment, and are more able to learn abstractions.

It also follows that the genes that control the pruning process are genes that control other developmental processes, such as growth of the body in general. Once these genes tell the body to stop maturing, the pruning process is turned off as well. In other words, the genome does not have different genes to independently control these processes.

This implies that the only way the ability to understand could continue to grow in adulthood is if there was no maturity, and the body continued to grow throughout the lifespan. However, not only would too much stress be placed on muscles and bones if this was the case, but coordination would become difficult and various medical complications would result. This would far outweigh the advantage of the ability to understand continuing to develop.

Even if there were separate genes to turn off developmental processes in the brain versus the rest of the body, there may still be complications. The pruning process involves initially producing an abundance of neural connections. However, the skull does not increase in size in adulthood. Having the neural connections continue to increase in adulthood could lead to the brain running out of space in the skull, resulting in brain damage. Continuing to lose connections throughout adulthood could also lead to problems.[174]

Natural Selection is Less Important after Reproductive Age

Natural selection is based on the principle that genetic changes that increase an organism's likelihood of survival are more likely to be passed on. However, genes are passed on by reproduction. It follows that evolution is more concerned with genetic changes that provide an advantage up until reproductive age. Whether a person is more or less successful after they have reproduced matters less, because their genes have already been passed on to future generations.

One example of this is wisdom teeth. Most people know that wisdom teeth are teeth at the back of the jaw that usually appear between the ages of 17 and 25. Many people have genes that cause wisdom teeth to grow at an incorrect angle, impacting surrounding teeth and causing pain and infection. Because of this, it is common to remove wisdom teeth surgically.

Why do wisdom teeth cause so many problems? Some people have genes that reduce problems with wisdom teeth, and do not need surgery. So why doesn't everyone have these genes, especially since in the past, before modern medicine, infections from wisdom teeth could lead to death?

Problems with wisdom teeth remain prevalent because they occur after reproductive age is reached. This means that people who have these genes are likely to have passed them on before developing difficulties—especially in our evolutionary past, when children were conceived soon after their parents reached reproductive age. Similarly, many other disorders with a genetic basis that affect a major proportion of the population only appear in adulthood.

So, even if genes were present that extended the learning of understanding into adulthood, there would be no strong pressure for these genes to be passed on to future generations. This is especially true given that the average life span was much shorter in our evolutionary past, so the difference between learning only occurring to maturity and learning occurring throughout the lifespan would have been much less.

Differences in the ability to understand would also have been less important in a hunter-gatherer environment where our genes evolved. While the ability to understand simple abstractions such as predators would have been useful, there would have been ample time to understand these abstractions before maturity was reached. It is only in our modern technological environment with much more known structure that the ability to understand could become a lifelong learning process. So again, there would not have been strong evolutionary pressures in the past to enable understanding to be learned in adulthood.

A Sensitive Period Might be Good!!?!

We have already learned that different cortical areas undergo the pruning process at different times. Cortical areas responsible for processing information directly from the senses go through the pruning process in early childhood. Higher-order cortical areas responsible for processing information from these sensory areas go through the pruning process at a later age.

This provides an advantage. It means that higher-order cortical areas can adapt based on stable representations of lower-order features from the sensory cortical areas. This makes it easier for the higher-order cortical areas to learn abstractions or commonalities across experiences.

Similarly, having the higher-order cortical areas obtain stable representations leads to better memory. It means that configurations and sequences of stable abstractions can then be learned. If the connections continued to change, this would imply that the abstractions based on these connections would change as well. Memory based on the original abstractions would then be corrupted. Indeed, perhaps young adults are so adept at learning new configurations and sequences of abstractions compared to younger children precisely because their neural connections are no longer changing![175]

Moving On

Whatever the reason for the sensitive period, the evidence from psychological tests that assess understanding abstractions, as well as brain science and observations of our society, indicate that there is a difference between childhood and adulthood in learning to understand abstractions. Only by taking this difference into account can we enable children to reach their full potential.

CHAPTER EIGHT

HOW A CHILD
CAN BE A GENIUS

We now turn to the question of genius. The term *genius* refers to someone who has created very original and significant work in a domain. It is an accolade that many would like to receive. Examples include Albert Einstein, Leonardo Da Vinci, Mozart, Stephen Hawking and Bill Gates. There is no doubt that this is a very mixed group of people, and it is unlikely that there is any simple characteristic that they all have in common. However, can we find any characteristic that seems to be more common in geniuses, contributing to their accomplishments?

Is Genius Simply High IQ?

Given that acts of genius involve producing novel solutions or creations, a relationship with IQ would seem obvious. Recall that many IQ subtests and other tests of intelligence involve solving novel problems. This would seem to be similar to what geniuses do in a particular domain.

Geniuses are also often recognized as having a greater ability to understand the domain, especially when the domain requires abstractions to understand it. An obvious example is Albert Einstein. His theories were so abstract that many of his peers had difficulty understanding them. Even now, despite his theories being considered to be perhaps the greatest intellectual achievement in history, few people can really claim to understand what his theories were about.

This suggests that genius is perhaps simply a case of having an extremely high IQ. This would make sense if we adopt the homunculus perspective. Someone with a high IQ has a "little person" in their brain that is very good at understanding abstractions. This homunculus should then be good at understanding other abstractions it has not encountered before as well. In this case, a very high-IQ individual should be able to show great performance in many domains, ultimately exhibiting outcomes that are characteristic of genius.

However, ignoring the lack of explanation of this homunculus, this conceptualization is found to be not true when people with extremely high IQs are investigated.

Success of Children with Extreme IQs

Lewis Terman was an American psychologist who was interested in intelligence at the beginning of the twentieth century. He took the original Binet–Simon intelligence test and created the Stanford-Binet IQ test that is still used today.[176] Terman believed that those people with the highest IQs would be the most able to produce novel performances that are characteristic of genius.

Terman then undertook a massive study to find children who scored the highest on IQ tests. This involved examining the performance of some 250,000 elementary and high school students. From this huge group of children, he identified 1,470 students that had the highest IQs. These young "geniuses" were then followed for the rest of their lives, with the expectation that many from this group would become Nobel Prize winners, great composers, and famous artists.

So, how did it work out? Not as Terman expected. Given their high IQs, the "Termites" had the opportunity to enter some of the best colleges, as well as pass other stringent selection processes. Consequently, they certainly earned better than average incomes. However, what was stiking was that they were *not* exceptional. Their accomplishments were typical for people with their qualifications. They were not geniuses, or nationally renowned figures.[177]

This again suggests that IQ does not measure some mythical ability to solve any problem. If it did, then people with high IQs would be expected to be able to show genius across a wide range of domains. Instead, while people with extremely high IQs do well on the types of abstraction problems that are included in IQ tests, they do not necessarily do very well in other situations that involve abstractions.

Is Genius Simply Greater Experience?

K. Anders Ericsson has argued that there is no such thing as talent when it comes to various examples of expert performance, such as playing the violin, golf, or surgery.[178] He argues that expertise comes from what he describes as *deliberate practice*. Deliberate practice is when someone practices an activity not for fun, but with the specific aim of improving their performance.

The data he uses to support his conjecture is amazing. He estimates that the average professional violinist will have racked up over 10,000 hours of deliberate practice by the time they reach adulthood. This is a massive amount! If you conscientiously practiced for 2 hours a week every week for 10 years, you would only have accrued 1,000 hours of practice. To accumulate 10,000 hours of practice, professional violinists practice up to 30 hours per week over the course of several years. Remember this next time you see a professional violinist performing!

However, Ericsson went beyond the sheer number of hours of practice to make a number of other interesting observations. He observed that there is no such thing as *enough* practice. At the least, playing the violin can be viewed as making very complex and precise motor movements. Even for the best violinists, these motor movements are never completely perfect. There are always gains, or slight refinements to technique, that can be made. This means that a violinist never reaches a point whereby further practice does not lead to further improvement. Their practice will always be aimed at reducing the small errors that they are still making.

Ericsson also found that the perceived "talent" of a violinist seemed to be in direct proportion to the amount of practice they had undertaken. By adulthood, the most "talented" violinists had done at least 10,000 hours of practice, the average violinists had done 8,000 hours of practice, and the least "talented" violinists had done *just* 4,000 hours. This suggested that there was no such thing as "talent," only those who had done more or less practice.[179]

The Role of Deliberate Practice in Genius

The performances that Ericsson studied were quite different to the domains where genius is typically displayed. Ericsson's studies were concerned with performances that involved very fine motor control. Scientific studies suggest that these performances depend on a region of the brain other than the cerebral cortex, the region responsible for thinking.[180] Indeed, playing the violin is like many other examples of skilled performances, such as car racing and baseball, where events occur too quickly to consciously think about them. Trained performers in these domains develop very specialized reflexes such that they can produce the correct responses "automatically." These trained responses come about through the deliberate practice that was the subject of Ericsson's studies. They involve repeating the same situation over and over, slowly reducing reaction times and increasing accuracy.

On the other hand, acts of genius tend to consist not of repeated behaviors that are gradually refined over time, but rather novel or inventive responses that may have been the result of extensive thought or contemplation. Even so, can we use Ericsson's observations of extensive practice to explain genius?

If genius was simply the accrual of experience or practice, then you would expect that the elderly would be the most likely to show genius—as they have had the longest time in which to accrue experience. How could a 20-year-old ever compete with a 60-year-old? It would also be expected that the first evidence of genius would be shown late in life. It would take this long for an above-average amount of experience to be accrued.

However, this is not what is observed with genius. Harvey Lehman examined the ages of elite performers in many different domains, including mathematics, philosophy, literature, music, and art.[181] He observed that geniuses tend to be young when they demonstrate their greatest accomplishments. Most often, their greatest work will be performed between the ages of 20 and 30, and their performance will then decline as they get older.

This age range should not be surprising, as it corresponds to the time at which the ability to understand abstractions is at its peak. It suggests that being better able to understand is what leads to acts of genius. This is especially so when it is recognized that people of this age often do not have the resources granted to older adults, and have often only recently commenced work in their chosen profession. These impediments should make it extremely difficult for someone to make a major accomplishment at an early age, at least if genius is viewed as simply being a consequence of greater experience. This suggests that there is more to genius than just extensive experience.

IS GENIUS BEING IN THE RIGHT PLACE AT THE RIGHT TIME?

If genius is not simply due to high IQ or extensive experience, why is it that some people make huge contributions to our society while others lead ordinary lives? One contributing factor that has been ably described by Malcolm Gladwell is the combination of chance and circumstances.[182]

In short, making a significant contribution depends on being in the right place at the right time. People often win the Nobel Prize in science because they happen to be in a particular scientific field at a time when the methods or technology progress to the point that such a discovery is inevitable. Sometimes, it is known that the discovery is just around the corner, and many researchers are rushing to be the first to make the breakthrough.

However, as a beginning scientist, it can be difficult, if not impossible, to anticipate which field is likely to yield a Nobel Prize at the time when you are choosing your specialization. It is often luck that leads to a person being in the right discipline at the right time, resulting in a Nobel Prize-worthy breakthrough.

Gladwell identifies other factors outside a person's control that can also lead to success. One such factor is geography. It would have been difficult to become a billionaire in the IT boom if you were living in Tanzania. Being located in the US was almost essential, and being near Silicon Valley helped as well. Another factor is when you were born. Being born too soon can mean that you have decided to embark on an alternative career before a new groundbreaking opportunity has become evident. Being born too late can mean that you are too young to embark on the new career path while it is still "hot" and the potential for a breakthrough exists. It is about being in the right place at the right time.

However, many people fit the geographical and time requirements. What, then, determines who will be successful?

More Than Just The Right Place and The Right Time

Gladwell focuses on the case of Bill Gates, founder of Microsoft, and notes that Gates' success was due to his exceptional programming ability. Gladwell uses Ericsson's concept of 10,000 hours of practice to account for this ability. Gates was special in that he had the opportunity to gain programming experience on a mainframe computer while still in high school. At the time, this was very rare. Gates spent literally hours programming every night and every weekend, such that he had racked up 10,000 hours of programming experience by the time he graduated from high school. According to Gladwell, this huge amount of practice is what made Gates such an exceptional programmer.

However, Gladwell's argument does not make sense as it is presented. The reality is that 10,000 hours of practice is not that impressive. Consider the amount of practice or experience that one would get in a typical job; 40 hours per week x 50 weeks per year x 5 years = 10,000 hours. So Gladwell is arguing that anyone who has been a full-time programmer for 5 years has the same programming ability as Bill Gates!

The reality is very different. Computer programming is *hard*. If five years of experience was all it took to become equivalent to Bill Gates in programming ability, then companies would have no difficulty hiring wizard programmers. However, anyone in information technology knows that this is not the case. It is very difficult to find good programmers, even if they have years and years of experience. This is the reason that information technology salaries are so high.

Even more striking is that Gladwell's argument is not even supported by his own interview with Gates. Gladwell quotes Gates as attributing his success to "I had a better exposure to software development *at a*

188

young age than I think anyone did in that period of time..." (emphasis added).[183] So Gates was not just saying that the 10,000 hours of experience was important. The age at which it occurred was also important!

This is not surprising. After all, computer programming involves abstractions. It involves combining procedures into new configurations based on general principles, like the examples of intelligence test items we saw previously. If one is to understand the abstractions involved in computer programming as well as possible, it would make sense to learn these abstractions at the time when children are still increasing their ability to understand abstractions.

On the other hand, adults do not show an increasing ability to understand abstractions in general. They are then less likely to learn to understand the abstractions involved in computer programming. Instead, they will often rely on rote memorization of programming solutions that apply to specific contexts. They will have difficulty transferring these solutions to different contexts, or applying their knowledge flexibly to create novel solutions. While this will not prevent them from being able to program, they will not find it as easy or be as creative.

THE MISSING FACTOR TO GENIUS—CHILDHOOD EXPERIENCE

This suggests that childhood experience is essential for genius. If we then look at biographies of geniuses, we see that they typically do not suddenly demonstrate their great accomplishments in adulthood. Rather, geniuses in adulthood are also notable because they had an interest in the field or domain while they were young. Often, this is not just an interest, but an obsession.

189

This is consistent with Ericsson's finding that the amount of experience is crucial, but it is experience during childhood that is especially important. By showing an interest in the domain during childhood, geniuses obtain experiences that enable them to better understand relevant abstractions. On the other hand, someone who only gains experience in the domain in adulthood will have more difficulty genuinely understanding it. Let us consider some specific examples.

Examples of Genius

We have already talked about Bill Gates. Gates was able to be successful as a result of his programming ability, which enabled him to write the original operating system for personal computers. He had this programming ability because he obtained extensive programming experience while young, at a time when abstractions can still be learned.

Another example is Steven Spielberg.[184] Spielberg transformed the movie industry with original blockbusters like *Jaws* and *Close Encounters of the Third Kind*. He created these films in his twenties, once again contradicting the notion that proficiency is merely due to expertise gained as a result of years of experience. If it was, all the best movies would come from eighty-year-old directors.

However, was Steven Spielberg such a natural at filmmaking that he was able to create these films while in his twenties with no experience at all? Not at all. Steven Spielberg was fascinated with making films from age twelve—before the end of the sensitive period. Throughout his early teens, he made amateur 8mm "adventure" movies with his friends. By the age of sixteen, Spielberg had so much experience with filmmaking that he wrote and directed his first independent movie, a 140-minute science-fiction adventure called *Firelight*. This movie was shown in the local cinema.

Even though this was only a few years of experience, it was a few years of experience during the sensitive period. It would have made changes in neural connections that have benefited him throughout his lifelong career in moviemaking. On the other hand, if someone becomes interested in moviemaking in adulthood, even decades of experience may not result in the same changes in the neural connections.

What about Mozart, one of the most famous composers of all time.[185] Composing music is, in many ways, like the other examples of understanding we have talked about. As with tests of either abstraction or language, composing music involves combining elements in novel configurations, but based on constraints that limit the possibilities.

Consistent with this, Mozart was not an old man with decades of experience when he composed his greatest work. His best work was produced in his twenties, and he passed away at the age of 35. However, again, he did not just begin to compose once he had reached adulthood. He was renowned as being a prodigy who had begun to compose music from five years of age—although his early compositions were in no way special.[186]

This composing of music at age five was not necessarily a sign of exceptional talent, for Mozart's father was a composer and music teacher, and taught and encouraged his child from infancy. It may be that Mozart was born with certain talents, as well. However, would he have been such a great composer if he had first taken an interest and begun composing music at age twenty?

Another domain that involves composing novel creations is architecture. Possibly the most celebrated architect of all time is Frank Lloyd Wright.[187] Did Wright choose to become an architect at age twenty? Again, we find that Wright had extensive experience relevant to architecture during childhood. His mother had declared that her first child would grow up to build beautiful buildings, before he had even been born. To encourage this, she decorated his nursery with engravings of English cathedrals. She also bought him a set of geometrically-shaped educational blocks that could be assembled in various combinations to form three-dimensional compositions.

Wright later identified the influence of these blocks and exercises in childhood on his approach to design. Experience with these blocks enabled him to visualize novel configurations of three-dimensional structures. This was the hallmark of his distinctive style later on.

Finally, we cannot close this discussion without talking about Einstein. Einstein is often considered to be the greatest thinker of the last few generations.[188] He, too, advanced the theories for which he became famous when he was relatively young—his special theory of relativity was published when he was just 26, while his general theory of relativity was published when he was 37. Again, experience as reflected by age did not seem to be crucial.

Consistent with the other geniuses we have reviewed here, Einstein's childhood was also different to normal. There is evidence that he was gifted. However, rather than just following what was taught to him in school, he acquired a curiosity and was thinking about the underlying forces in the universe from the age of five. By twelve, he was studying advanced mathematics textbooks.

He even insisted that he had not been born with any special gift, just a capacity for unceasing reflection and contemplation that he possessed from an early age.[189] Again, this unceasing reflection and contemplation during childhood would have given his brain important experiences. It would have allowed his brain to develop the ability to understand abstractions that others who did not have these interests in childhood would not typically develop. He was able to use these abstractions later to develop his groundbreaking theories that explained the forces in the universe.

A New Rule

This suggests that Ericsson's rule of 10,000 hours of practice needs to be amended if it is to apply to domains that involve thinking or the understanding of abstractions. Rather than 10,000 hours of experience at any age, it is experience *in childhood* that is especially important.

Further, in contrast to past claims about the importance of very early childhood, it is *later* childhood experience that is likely to be most important. In very early childhood, children are learning simple abstractions such as speech recognition. Typically all children develop these skills eventually, so early experience with them is not important for ultimate attainment.

On the other hand, what differs across adults are typically the abstractions that are learned in later childhood. The brain areas responsible for these abstractions are often not even active in very young children. It is in adolescence that the brain goes through the pruning process to enable the learning of these abstractions. This suggests that *late* childhood environmental experience has the most importance in determining a person's future success.

Of course, acts of genius are also dependent on other factors, such as being in the right place at the right time, so merely being interested in a domain before maturity is no guarantee of success. However, if a child wants to be successful in a domain, then experience before maturity will not harm them, and it could give them an advantage in understanding the domain that will benefit them throughout their adult life.

CHAPTER NINE

WHAT IT MEANS FOR CHILDHOOD EDUCATION

This book began by arguing that we need to understand what causes differences in intelligence if children are to be helped as effectively as possible. Psychology has attempted in the past to define intelligence in terms of behavior, such as performance on intelligence tests. However, defining intelligence in this way has led to a lack of success. Behaviors are an outcome of intelligence, not a cause. Instead, examining intelligence reveals that it requires *understanding abstractions*. Therefore, any satisfactory explanation of intelligence needs to explain what abstractions are and how they are able to be understood.

It was then observed that identifying or perceiving abstractions is not simple. The challenge of getting computers to identify abstractions and

195

the performance of many adults on tests of abstraction illustrate this. While the process of identifying abstractions may seem easy to those who can understand the abstraction, it actually requires filtering out the information that changes from one concrete instance of the abstraction to the next. Only by filtering out this information can similarity be seen between what would otherwise be different situations.

We then learned that there is no automatic way that the brain can filter out this information. Neurons are not switches that can turn inputs or information on and off based on what information is being fed into the brain at the current time. There is also no homunculus or little person in the brain who can direct this turning on and off of inputs, thereby being the actual cause of "intelligent" behavior. So it is unrealistic to imagine the brain shaping or changing its activation around the network in real time in response to requirements, thereby forming different abstractions.

However, the brain can gradually learn to do this filtering out through experience. Neurons can filter out information by physically changing their connections so that only neurons that carry relevant information for an abstraction have connections with other neurons.

Recent evidence from brain science has shown that this is what the human brain does during childhood. The brain initially creates more connections than are needed. It then prunes those connections that are not used repeatedly, based on many, many experiences. This results in filtering out information that is unique to particular concrete instances. The connections that are retained are those that are used repeatedly across situations. This is a characteristic of abstractions or general principles that are present in the environment.

This indicates that the increasing ability to understand abstractions over childhood is due to a learning process. Childhood experience gives the brain information about patterns that repeat in the environment, and the neural connections in the brain then change to be more sensitive to these patterns. This is a slow process, and is the reason that children need many examples and much time to learn abstractions that seem obvious to adults.

However, once the connections have been pruned so that they more accurately reflect the general patterns present in the environment, these general patterns or abstractions can be immediately perceived when experienced. In this way, the adult brain has the ability to understand a huge number of different abstractions and is much more specialized than the child's brain. However, it takes many, many years of training and experience to make the adult brain the way it is.

Adults, then, can quickly learn new configurations and sequences of these abstractions that they learned to understand through childhood experience. This is shown by their knowledge and expertise about the world continuing to increase throughout life. Indeed, adults are much more capable of quickly learning new configurations or sequences of abstractions than children, as they can already understand a wider range of abstractions because of their past childhood experience.

However, adults find learning to understand new abstractions more difficult. This is reflected by the finding that performance on psychological tests that measure the ability to understand increases over childhood but not adulthood. It is also reflected by evidence that the process responsible for learning abstractions is more active in the developing brain than the adult brain. This means that there are certain situations where a child can do better, although the process of learning an abstraction can take a long time and require much experience. Essentially, childhood experience gives a person the mental "toolkit" of abstractions that they can

197

use to understand and predict the environment throughout their later life.

THE NEED TO BE TRUTHFUL

The occurrence of a sensitive period supports the old adage that children have a greater capacity to learn than adults, or that you "cannot teach an old dog new tricks". However, it is important to realize that this ability to learn is concerned with abilities that have traditionally been thought of as innate, or not due to learning at all.

While a sensitive period for learning these abilities can be seen as undesirable, this does not mean that this information should not be communicated. Irrespective of whether children and adults are told of the sensitive period, at least some children will receive appropriate experiences in childhood. By making the concept of a sensitive period more well-known, it can be ensured that both parents and children are better informed about the importance of childhood experience and education. Steps can then be taken to try and ensure that all children receive appropriate experiences.

In contrast, if people do not know about the sensitive period, children may not receive appropriate stimulation as its importance is not appreciated. This could lead to an adult having long-term difficulties with abstractions that they could have learned easily if they were given appropriate experiences in childhood. Only by recognizing the limitations that biology places on the brain can we ensure that people are able to approach their full potential.

One may compare the situation with an analogy from medicine. If evidence of a new disease is found, doctors do not suppress this information because it represents bad news for sufferers. Information about the disease is widely disseminated, especially if there are actions that people can undertake to avoid getting the disease themselves. Exactly the same is true for the sensitive period.

Many adults also already implicitly accept their limitations. They are realistic, and know that they could not enroll in an advanced quantum mechanics course at college and get an "A" for the course. However, this book is arguing that this inability may not be an innate limitation, it represents a deficit in childhood experience—a deficit that could be corrected for current and future children.

GENES AND ENVIRONMENT

Understanding how the brain produces intelligence also has implications for the debate over the role of genes and environment in intelligence. This debate has typically been polarized into two camps. One side will argue that differences in intelligence are due to the genes, or nature. The other side will argue that differences in intelligence are due to the environment, or nurture. The key point is that *both* differences in the genes and differences in the environment determine intelligence.

There are differences between people in the brain's capacity to adapt its connections to the environment. These differences would likely be genetic. However, this difference is not an "ability" in itself that directly allows someone to solve any intelligence problem. Rather, it is a potential to develop the appropriate neural connections given appropriate experiences. Appropriate experiences are then necessary for the brain to be able to change its neural connections so that it can perceive or understand abstractions. In this way, both genes and the environment contribute to the ability to understand.

This means that a person who demonstrates high intelligence by demonstrating an ability to understand many abstractions is like a trained elite athlete. Sure, they may have had a brain that could more easily learn abstractions, like a runner who has the right muscles to run fast. However, someone who is born with the right muscles to run fast will not automatically win an Olympic gold medal. They only have the potential. It is through years and years of training that these advantageous characteristics can be converted into an actual *ability* to run fast.

It is the same for the brain. Having a brain that can adapt its connections to the environment well so that it can identify abstractions does not mean that it will do this without experience. It is only with appropriate experience that the brain will get the right information that enables its connections to change.

Typically, children will rely on school to get this experience. The years and years of school experience enables the child's brain to develop the right connections to perceive or understand many abstractions. If a child has great potential in terms of giftedness but then does not work hard at school, they will not convert this potential into actual high intellectual performance. On the other hand, children who are less gifted but work harder can reach comparable intellectual levels. Children who develop interests outside of school that lead to relevant experiences can have an even greater chance of success.

Differences in Understanding

This brings us to a related issue. It is striking just how large the differences in the ability to understand are.

Even at college, where admission is based on tests that assess the ability to understand, there are still large differences across students. Some bright students will have no difficulty understanding everything a professor teaches, and will go on to develop new theories that make a major contribution to the field. Other students will struggle to understand the basic concepts in introductory courses and may not be able to pass their degree, despite putting in as much work as the other students.

The differences in ability to understand are even greater when the entire population is considered. While some exceptional individuals are inventing new technologies and adding to human knowledge, others in the population can be struggling with basic arithmetic and reading skills.

Why are there such large differences across the population in the ability to understand? Would evolution not predict that such large differences in intelligence would be subject to natural selection, such that those with a relatively low level of understanding would be less likely to survive? Would this not mean that differences in intelligence across the population would be reduced over generations?

One observation we can make is that the ability to understand likely only has a great impact on a person's life in modern society. In a hunter-gatherer society, the environment involved less understanding. It would have been valuable to know what foods are edible and ways to avoid predators, but it would not have been valuable to have the potential to understand something like calculus, much less quantum mechanics. So a greater ability to understand would have been less useful in the relatively simpler environment that existed while our species was evolving.

201

However, we can make another observation as well. School is a relatively recent phenomenon. Schooling provides children with years and years of experience with abstractions, enabling their neural connections to learn to perceive or understand them. This intensive environment that focuses on changing the neural connections would highlight differences in the ability to change these connections.

On the other hand, if two children with different IQs or potentials are born and brought up in a more primitive community, large differences in intelligence would not be as evident. It may not be readily known which of the children is more "intelligent." Indeed, the concept of intelligence itself may be very different to what it is in a population that is schooled.[190]

So, the large differences in intelligence that exist now are because the modern child's environment is very different to what it was in our evolutionary past—especially compared with the hunter-gatherer environment where our genes evolved.

Differences in Thinking

This concept of understanding being due to a learning process, and the role of school in producing large differences in understanding, emphasizes another characteristic of children who do better at school. While gifted children may find school easier, they also tend to work *harder* at school. This gives their brain greater experience, and makes them more able to understand abstractions.

What is meant by this? Any person who did well at school will be able to relate to the following statement; "I didn't understand it initially, but I kept *thinking* and *thinking* about it until eventually I got it." This represents an unwillingness to let something be beyond them, and even an ambition to be as smart as possible.

All this *thinking* and *thinking* gives the brain many more experiences of the abstraction that the child is having difficulty understanding. This experience then gives the neural connections the necessary information they need to prune effectively so that the abstraction can be seen or perceived.

On the other hand, consider how weaker students handle the same situation. If they have difficulty understanding something, they will not keep *thinking* and *thinking* about it. Instead, they will give up trying to understand it. They will then avoid trying to solve problems that involve this abstraction in the future. They have decided it is too hard for them.

Imagine what this means for brains that depend on many, many experiences with an abstraction in order to learn to understand it. If one child is thinking about the abstraction hundreds or even thousands of times, and another child has stopped thinking about the abstraction after just a few attempts, is it any surprise that there are such large differences in the ability to understand?

It is like the difference between gifted athletes and normal people. Sure, people may be born with differences in the ability to run fast. However, if gifted athletes spend years and years of training while average runners do no training at all, then whatever differences existed at birth will be much greater by adulthood. On the other hand, if all children did the same amount of running training, then differences in running ability will be much smaller.

This tells us that not only do all children need to go to school, but they need to put in the same amount of *effort* if differences in the ability to understand are not to be magnified. While schooling can provide appropriate materials, it is ultimately up to children themselves whether they take advantage of these materials. A teacher can go over concrete examples of an abstraction in the classroom repeatedly, but if a weaker student is not paying attention, this will make a major difference to the amount of experience that their brain is exposed to.

However, better students not only pay attention and accumulate experience in the classroom, they go beyond this. They memorize concrete instances using their auto-associative network, and then use this memory to repeatedly recall and go over the concrete examples in their mind outside of the classroom. Every time they recall the concrete instance, the elements that represent general principles or abstractions are further reinforced. This speeds up the process by which neurons in their brain can prune their connections, enabling them to actually see or perceive the underlying abstractions.

What this emphasizes is that children need to be told that understanding depends on effort. *Thinking during childhood* leads to a better ability to understand.

Cultural Differences in Effort and Persistence

Consistent with the effect of working hard in childhood, differences in IQ have also been related to cultural differences in effort and persistence. For instance, it is found that Asian people score higher on IQ tests than Whites.[191] Does this mean that Asians are born smarter than Whites?

Not necessarily. What about the stereotypes of these cultures? Is an Asian or a White student more likely to be a "nerd," always listening to the teacher and completing all of their homework? We all know that Asians tend to be more conscientious when it comes to school work. This greater effort is related to their culture, which emphasizes that success is based on hard work.[192] Reflecting this, it is estimated that Japanese high school students do an average of 3.5 hours of study per day. American high school students do an average of only 1.5 hours of study per day![193]

The difference between Asians and Whites has also been shown in psychological studies. In one study, Japanese and Canadian students were asked to do a creativity test. After a certain time, they were told that they either did well or poorly on the test—independent of how they had really performed. The participants were then given a similar test and told to work on it for as long as they wanted. The Canadians worked longer on the second creativity test if they had been told that they had done well on the first creativity test. For the Japanese, the reverse was found. They worked longer on the second test if they had been told that they had done *poorly* on the first test![194]

Similarly, what if an Asian student and a White student are given a very challenging problem to solve? Again, there will be marked differences in their behavior. On average, the White student will only persevere with the problem for a few minutes and then give up. On the other hand, the Asian student will be much more persistent. They will continue working on the problem for hours in the hope of eventually solving it.[195]

Given the difference that experience makes to the neural connections, is it any wonder that there are differences in IQ between Asians and Whites? Or that Asians perform better than Whites on tests of mathematics and science? In short, all of the hard work in childhood does ultimately pay off, not because it leads to increased knowledge—which can be learned quite quickly in adulthood anyway—but because it leads to better understanding.

HELPING CHILDREN TO REACH THEIR FULL POTENTIAL

How may we use this integration of intelligence research with brain science to improve intelligence? We have noted that the genetic factor that contributes to the ability to understand is not an ability in itself. It is only the potential to change the neural connections given appropriate experiences in childhood. IQ is a measure of this potential.

However, in order to understand abstractions, appropriate experiences are required as well. Contradicting the belief that geniuses are just born, every genius or high achiever has also received extensive experience in the domain that led to their achievements.

This means that a gifted child with no experience of abstractions from a relevant domain will perform worse than a less-gifted child who has had extensive experience with relevant abstractions. In some ways, this concept is most similar to Gardner's multiple intelligences, whereby the ability to adapt to and understand the environment can be channeled into many different domains. Some are domains that are readily taught at school. However, there are other domains that are not catered for by schools at present.

Since it requires so much time or experience in a domain to be successful, it also follows that it is impossible for a child to get sufficient experience in childhood to cover every domain. No child can excel at everything. A person with a lower IQ who has spent extensive time in a domain is therefore likely to do better than a higher-IQ person who has gained little suitable experience in childhood. So, being interested in a domain and studying it while young will be of benefit, irrespective of a person's IQ.

Learning Abstractions

This raises the question of what abstractions exist, and which situations they are required for. Some abstractions apply across many domains. For instance, the ability to represent information in formulas and apply mathematical operations can play a major role in many fields and occupations. This includes not only mathematics, but also biology, psychology, engineering, architecture, and medicine, to name a few. This suggests that it is critical that as many children as possible learn to understand mathematical abstractions.

However, there are other abstractions that are more specific to particular domains. Obvious examples would include architecture, music, and art. How may children learn the abstractions in these different domains?

The child should be given access to materials that will give them examples and descriptions of the domain in which they are interested. Books are often a good source of this information. Books have the advantage that they are much more detailed than other information mediums such as television. In addition, children can read through the book at their own pace. This lets them go through difficult sections repeatedly—giving them the required repetition that is necessary to enable them to gradually understand the abstractions that underlie the domain.

It is also helpful for a child to obtain some practical experience with the domain. This can be done by visiting museums, technology centers, and open days at universities.

More generally, a child should be brought up in a setting that encourages them to think about the world. They should try to work out the answers to problems for themselves. If they are still unable to solve a problem, they should be given hints that again encourage them to think about the problem. It is much better if they work something out for themselves by repeatedly thinking about it than if they are simply told the answer and memorizing it.

Parents should also give reasons—or the general principles underlying their statements—for any decisions they make. They should also describe the abstractions that make up the world. While general principles can be learned through exposure alone, language provides information about general principles that have already been identified through experience by other people. This allows abstractions to be learned more quickly.

Teachers should also not assume that their students can understand abstractions just because they can understand them. There is a tendency for teachers to learn material and then believe that they can quickly transfer this knowledge to their students. If students are having difficulty with the material, it is believed that the students are poor or not working hard enough. In reality, students may not be getting the material because they do not understand the same abstractions that the teacher does. The curriculum should also be altered so that children are given enough time to learn new abstractions.

The Role of Thinking

However, even more important than the environment that is presented to the child, it is important to instill in the child a recognition of the importance of thinking about the world for themselves. It is through thinking about the world that the brain obtains information about abstractions, learning to perceive and understand them.

This means that it is essential to *tell* the child about the sensitive period. This tells them that the work they put in during childhood will reward them in the future. This is especially effective in later childhood, when children are more likely to be learning abstractions that other children may not learn. It is most effective at this time because the child is older. This means that the child is more likely to recognize the importance of hard work, and the value of making sacrifices now in order to achieve future success.

Unfortunately, there is no shortcut to avoid this. If a child does not make a conscious effort to work hard at school and to think about what they are being taught, they will not succeed—no matter how good the teacher and school facilities are. On the other hand, many successful adults have come from quite impoverished school environments. They were still able to succeed because they worked hard in those environments.

The role of repetition should also be explained to children so that they can understand the need for schooling to be repetitive, rather than thinking that this repetition is needless. For instance, children will often complain about having to learn quadratic equations or Pythagoras' theorem, and they will not see the use of having to repeat 50 of these same math problems. They will view these formulas and repetitions as pointless, believing that they will not use them in their adult life.

Ironically, children are often *correct* in this belief. How many adults really use quadratic equations or Pythagoras' theorem? It is not surprising that parents and teachers have such a difficult time justifying school work to many children.

What children should be told is that it is not the specific formula that is important, but the abstractions that enable formulas to be used. Once these abstractions are mastered, then formulas representing many characteristics of the environment may be used. It is then easy to demonstrate how formulas are essential in so many careers and domains. Children should also be told that learning to use formulas is an ability that will stay with them long after they have forgotten the specific formulas themselves. It will mean that when they are shown a formula in adulthood, they will automatically be able to use it successfully.

By having these realities explained to them, children can be motivated to work hard at school as they can see how it is an investment in their future—their hard work will benefit them in the long run. On the other hand, by not informing children about the sensitive period for learning the ability to understand, they will be less motivated to work hard during childhood. This can mean that they fail to fulfill their potential.

THE FUTURE

This book has an important message. While it is easy to claim that everyone has the potential to do anything they put their mind to, this is not what is found in school, in college, and in the workplace. The reality is that understanding is *hard*. There are no easy fixes or quick solutions.

Brain science suggests that improving intelligence is possible, but it is more likely to occur if children are given the right experiences at the right ages. This does not mean that it is impossible to learn to understand abstractions at other ages, but the evidence suggests that it is likely to be more difficult. Adults can get around this by simply memorizing correct responses. However, memorization is less flexible and leads to less creativity than understanding underlying abstractions.

Ideally, the educational process should be shaped by how the brain learns. This includes the notion that the role of school is to train the neural connections to understand abstractions, and identifying those abstractions that are essential to be understood. This is in contrast to the present where no differentiation is made in school between different types of information that are being taught, or recognition that the brain is more prepared to learn certain types of information at certain ages.

However, because of the politically sensitive nature of human intelligence, researchers and money continue to be distributed away from the field. This means that little progress has been made in the past. Unless this is changed, further progress in understanding human intelligence is likely to continue to be slow. This will continue to hinder educational outcomes.

ENDNOTES

1   Albert Einstein is not known to have taken an IQ test, so this is just an estimate based on his achievements. Later in this book we will examine just how sufficient IQ is in explaining the accomplishments of someone like Einstein.

2   Gardner, 1993.

3   Binet & Simon, 1916, 1973, pp. 42-43.

4   Wechsler, 1944, p. 3.

5   Jensen, 1980, p. 249.

6   Herrnstein & Murray, 1994.

7   Gottfredson, 1997.

8   Sternberg, 1985, p. 45.

9   Gardner, 1993, p. xx.

10   Gardner, 1993, p. x.

11   Of course, someone may not understand something because it has not yet been explained to them or it has been explained poorly. However, once a sufficient explanation has been given, people can differ in their ability to "understand" it.

12   Snyderman & Rothman, 1987.

13   Flavell, 1963; Miller, 1993; Piaget, 1952.

14   Bolles, 1993.

15   Hebb, 1949.

16   Carroll, 1993.

17   The correct answer for the last item is B. Note that these items are not identical to the items on the actual Raven's Progressive Matrices test.

18   Gottfredson, 2002; Jensen, 1998; Park, Lubinski & Benbow, 2008; Schmidt & Hunter, 2004.

19   Bartholomew, 2004; Carroll, 1993; Jensen, 1998; Spearman, 1904.

20   Indeed, as you will see later, the framework introduced in this book does quite easily allow for these exceptions.

21   Flavell, 1963; Miller, 1993; Piaget, 1952.

22 Cattell, 1987; Horn, 1998. This lack of increase is found even for individuals that lead very intellectually-stimulating adult lives, although there is some evidence that mental exercise in adulthood can reduce the decline in later life.

23 Nisbett, 2009.

24 Kaufman & Lichtenberger, 2006.

25 This indicates that just hearing someone's IQ score obscures a lot of information about how performance on IQ tests changes over the lifespan. This lack of information has likely impeded an explanation of IQ by researchers from other fields who are unfamiliar with how IQ tests really work.

26 The curves in this figure are intended to mirror the IQ curve in Figure 2. However, the exact curving has been omitted to ease the illustration.

27 Jensen, 1980; Moffitt, Caspi, Harkness, & Silva, 1993; Wilson, 1983.

28 Brody, 1992; Jensen, 1998; Mackintosh, 1998.

29 This analogy was taken from Pinel, 2007.

30 While differences in language may not account for differences in performance on an IQ test when everyone has the same language background, this does not preclude differences in language affecting performance when there are differences in language background.

31 Plomin, 1990.

32 For instance, Mackintosh (1986, p. 2) notes that "A useful antidote for those who think that a high heritability for IQ would carry political implications of the most reactionary nature is to note that, on the contrary, it is plausibly a mark of a just society... The higher the heritability, therefore, the fewer the relevant environmental differences between members of the population."

33 Carey, 2003.

34 Jensen, 1998.

35 See Shattuck, 1980, for a discussion of the Wild Boy of Aveyron. See Curtis, 1977, for a discussion of Genie.

36 Boomsma, Busjahn, & Peltonen, 2002; Johnson, Turkheimer, Gottesman, & Bouchard, 2009.

37 Bouchard, 1997; Loehlin, Horn, & Willerman, 1997; Plomin, 1999.

38 Neisser et al., 1996. See also Nisbett, 2009.

39 Bouchard, 1997; Herrnstein & Murray, 1994; Jensen, 1998.

40 Bouchard, in press; Haworth et al., in press.

41 Streissguth, Barr, Sampson, Darby, & Martin, 1989.

42 Baumeister & Bacharach, 1996; Mackintosh, 1998.

43 Dunn & Plomin, 1990.

44 Eysenck & Schoenthaler, 1997.

45 Chabris et al., 1999; Roth & Smith, 2008; Thompson, Schellenberg & Husain, 2001.

46 Snow, 1995.

47 Jensen, 1998; Spearman, 1904.

48 McDaniel, 2005; Wickett, Vernon, & Lee, 2000.

49 Skoyles, 1999.

50 Muter, Taylor, & Vargha-Khadem, 1997.

51 Colom, Jung, & Haier, 2006; Pol et al., 2006.

52 Eysenck, 1994; Jensen, 2006; Sheppard & Vernon, 2008.

53 Deary, 2003.

54 Rijsdijk, Boomsma, & Vernon, 1995; Wickett & Vernon, 1994.

55 Kane & Engle, 2002; Kyllonen & Christal, 1990.

56 Ackerman, Beier, & Boyle, 1995.

57 Kyllonen, personal correspondence.

58 Working memory capacity can then be seen as a theoretical soup stone when it comes to explaining intelligence (Navon, 1984). The term soup stone comes from the Brothers Grimm folk tale. Hungry travelers arrive at a town with no money or food. All they have is a soup pot. They put a stone in the soup pot, fill it with water, and place it over a fire. They claim that the stone alone will result in a delicious soup. The villagers are curious about the soup. However, when they try it, they find that it lacks taste. The travelers say that the stone really does produce delicious soup, but a few vegetables are needed to bring out the flavor. The villagers dutifully add the vegetables, wanting to see just how delicious stone soup can be. After adding the vegetables, the taste is still not great. The travelers then say to add some meat as well, and some spices. Sure enough, eventually the stone soup does indeed taste delicious. However, it is not because of the stone. If the stone was not present, the eventual soup would have tasted just the same. This is like the working memory capacity explanation for intelligence. Working memory capacity is an intervening variable that can be invoked whenever "thinking" tasks are being described. However, it does not explain these thinking tasks itself. Other mechanisms are required. And once these other mechanisms are included, working memory capacity is likely to not provide any additional explanatory value. The construct itself can then be eliminated.

59 Jaeggi et al., 2008.

60 Moody, 2009.

61   Brody, 1992; Deary, 2000; Detterman, 1994; Jensen, 1998; Neisser et al., 1996; Nisbett, 2009.

62   Mountcastle, 1998; Stirling, 2000.

63   Changeux, 1985; Deacon, 1990; Preuss, 2000.

64   Luria, 1966; Martin, Ungerleider, & Haxby, 2000.

65   Damasio, 1990.

66   Karnath, Milner & Vallar, 2002.

67   It has been shown that the pre-frontal cortex plays an especially important role in some abstractions tasks, such as Raven's Progressive Matrices. The pre-frontal cortex is also one of the last cortical regions to develop. However, it is only the most difficult Raven's problems that are dependent on the pre-frontal cortex, indicating that other Raven's problems depend on other cortical areas that develop earlier (Duncan et al., 2000).

68   Corballis, 1999.

69   Beyerstein, 1999; Kalat, 2007.

70   Roder, Rosler, & Neville, 2000; Tierney, Varga, Hosey, Grafman, & Braun, 2001.

71   Goodman & Whitaker, 1985; Vicari et al., 2000.

72   Erbas, Meinertzhagen, & Shaw, 1991.

73   Calvin, 1995; Edelman & Tononi, 2000.

74   Abeles, Prut, Bergman, & Vaadia, 1994; Kritzer & Goldman-Rakic, 1995; Uylings, Van Pelt, Parnavelas, & Ruiz-Marcos, 1994.

75   Carlson, 2009.

76   Rovee-Collier, 1999.

77   Williams & Herrup, 1988.

78   Eriksson et al., 1998; Gould et al., 1999; Wiskott, Rasch & Kempermann, 2006).

79   Churchland & Sejnowski, 1992; Elman et al., 1996; McLeod, Plunkett, & Rolls, 1998; O'Reilly & Munakata, 2000; Rumelhart & McClelland, 1986.

80   Rakic, 1995.

81   Antonini & Stryker, 1993; Fuster, 1995; O'Donnell, Noseworthy, Levine, & Dennis, 2005; Rakic, 1995.

82   International Human Genome Sequencing Consortium, 2004.

83   Chimpanzee Sequencing and Analysis Consortium, 2005.

84   Gierer & Muller, 1995; Levitt, 2000; Polleux, 2005.

85   Dayhoff, 1990; Oppenheim, Skerry, Tramo, & Gazzaniga, 1989.

86   The differences in the connections across people can be used to debunk a few myths. For instance, in science-fiction, it is often claimed that a person's identity

and memory could be transferred from one brain to another. Given that every brain is different in its connections, any memory would become different once transferred. Also, reading someone's mind, or mental telepathy, would be difficult. Even if you know what neurons are active in a person's brain, you would not know what this means without knowing how all of their neurons are connected.

87 Berlucchi & Buchtel, 2009; Black & Greenough, 1986; Poldrack, 2000; Singer, 1995.

88 Hubel & Wiesel, 1979.

89 Hirsch & Spinelli, 1971.

90 Pettigrew & Freeman, 1973.

91 It is striking just how much neuroscience has changed in the last few decades. Greenough et al. (1993, p. 173) observed that "That the brain is plastic to experience in all these dimensions is nearly universally accepted among neuroscientists today; in the late 60s and early 70s, such concepts were radical or revolutionary and data such as those presented here were widely disbelieved."

92 Hensch, 2004; Johnston et al., 2009; Uylings, 2006.

93 Huttenlocher, 1990.

94 Fine et al., 2003; Ostrovsky, Meyers, Ganesh, Mathur & Sinha (in press); Valvo, 1971. Similar observations are made with auditory input (Sharma, Nash & Dorman, 2009).

95 Hata et al., 2000; O'Leary, 1996; Price, Lotto, Warren, Magowan, & Clausen, 1995; Van Veen & Van Pelt, 1994; Zhou & Black, 2000.

96 This process has been described in the literature as a "competitive" process as the neurons will compete to successfully make connections. Those that lose the competition will eventually die.

97 Erwin, Obermayer, & Schulten, 1995; Swindale, 1996.

98 It is sometimes argued that simulation evidence is unimportant as the observed outcome is the intended goal of the simulation. However, when the simulation simulates an underlying process, it is the underlying process that determines the outcome. Only if the underlying process is a sufficient explanation of the observed outcome will the simulation work. Hence, simulation shows that an underlying process is a sufficient explanation but not necessarily the actual explanation.

99 This is different to the process whereby people become more sensitive to differences in stimuli through exposure. This process is referred to as perceptual learning (Seitz & Dinse, 2007). Examples include wine connoisseurs and bird watchers. Perceptual learning differs because it involves identifying differences between

similar stimuli rather than treating different stimuli as the same. Perceptual learning is also a process that is active throughout the lifespan.

100 Morrison & Hof, 1997.

101 Bradmetz, 1999.

102 Squire (2004) gives a good summary of the different types of memory that have been identified in the psychological literature so far but, strikingly, the pruning process is not listed.

103 Our memory for events tends to also be better if the memory is distinctive (Hunt & Worthen, 2006). For instance, you may have been to hundreds of parties, but the one party you will always remember is the one where someone fell in the pool. If our memory depended on the process described in this chapter, then remembering the distinctive party would be the most difficult as it has the least in common with other parties.

104 Huttenlocher & Dabholkar, 1997; Mrzljak, Uylings, Van Eden & Judas, 1990; O'Donnell, Noseworthy, Levine, & Dennis, 2005.

105 Bourgeois, Goldman-Rakic, and Rakic (2000, p. 47-48) stated that "As adulthood is the most prolonged period of primate life and adult synaptogenesis is of great interest, we have examined several thousand photomicrographs in search of ultrastructural evidence of new synaptic connections or their turnover during this period. While we observed growth cones and immature types of contacts or degenerating forms of connections during the formative stages (phases 1-4), we failed to observe any of these markers of new synaptic connections during this three-decade period of adult life."

106 Caruso, Taylor & Detterman, 1982; Jensen, 1969; Spitz, 1999.

107 Garlick, 2002, 2003.

108 This is a key concept. The top figure showing the development of the ability to understand abstractions over childhood could be used to describe the development of individual abstractions. A number of figures like this will show that a person who develops the ability to understand abstractions faster will be better across a range of tasks that involve abstractions. In other words, a positive correlation across the tasks will be found, suggesting a general factor of intelligence (Jensen, 1998).

109 Since the neural connections stop developing at maturity, whatever differences exist at that age remain in adulthood. However, it is also likely that many abstractions seem "harder" not because they are, but because children are less likely to receive the necessary environmental stimulation. For instance, language involves

difficult abstractions, but most children master language very well. This could be because the amount of language stimulation is much greater than stimulation for many other abstractions that people find more "difficult".

110 A clear example of this incorrect assumption is given by Nisbett (2009). He describes these types of problems as "on-the-spot reasoning." He then gives the example of asking what is in common between forgiveness and revenge (p. 52). It is claimed that these problems represent "on-the-spot reasoning" because you have likely never before been asked this question or been given the correct answer. However, this does not mean that you are solving it "on-the-spot." In childhood, you would have experienced many concrete examples of both forgiveness and revenge. Through *exposure alone*, your neural connections would have extracted the commonality between these two events—that they both involve someone being wronged. So you already know that these two events have a common element before you are explicitly asked what it is. Asking the question is just giving you the opportunity to reveal what you have already learned through past experience.

111 Of course, the different context ensures that successfully solving the problem does actually require an understanding of the abstraction. If it was the same context, then correctly answering the problem could be based on having seen the exact same problem and answer before and memorizing the solution.

112 The challenge in explaining g has always been that people do better on problems that require different algorithms for their solution. This is one reason why explanations such as working memory capacity are not satisfactory. If it was plausible that different tests of abstraction could be solved by a single mechanism, then g would not be such a perplexing finding in the first place. On the other hand, the current explanation allows different tasks to be based on different algorithms for their solution. At the same time, these different algorithms are related, as they all develop through the same developmental mechanism.

113 Jensen, 1969.

114 Garlick, 2002, has neural network simulations that show that a low rate of learning can result in such slow acquisition that even large differences in experience do not alter the course of development. In this way, the developmental process can seem to be not due to environmental experience.

115 Nisbett, 2009.

116 Brody, 1992; Jensen, 1998; Mackintosh, 1998.

117 Bindu & Dharmangadan, 2007; Mayes, Calhoun, Bixler & Zimmerman, 2009.

118 Ceci (1996) notes that Brazilian street children have excellent arithmetical skills despite a lack of formal education. However, these skills are still acquired through extensive experience, not just formal schooling. This still supports the view that experience is necessary to acquire these abstractions.

119 Jensen, 1998; Mayes, Calhoun, Bixler & Zimmerman, 2009.

120 In this way, heritability estimates are ambiguous regarding the underlying cause of a characteristic. The heritability of a characteristic will be the same whether the trait develops without environmental stimulation, or develops with environmental stimulation that is the same across people. Other evidence, such as evidence from brain science, is needed to determine what causes the development.

121 In some cases, highly g-loaded tasks are specifically chosen. In other cases, such as IQ tests, tasks are chosen where all children are likely to have received the necessary environmental stimulation. Either way, as we will see, heritability will be exaggerated.

122 Garlick, 2002.

123 Jensen (1998, p. 169) states that "the relative g loadings of various tests predict their relative heritability coefficients."

124 As incredible as this position sounds, some researchers do advocate it. For instance, Pinker (1994, pp. 93, 97) argues that "It is a certain wiring of the microcircuitry that is essential... If language, the quintessential higher cognitive process, is an instinct, maybe the rest of cognition is a bunch of instincts too—complex circuits designed by natural selection, each dedicated to solving a particular family of computational problems posed by the ways of life we adopted millions of years ago." See also Buss, 1999; Tooby & Cosmides, 1995; Wilson, 1975.

125 This view has been termed neoteny in the literature. See Bjorklund, 1997; Changeux, 1985; Gould, 1977.

126 Jensen, 1998.

127 Ceci, 1991; Nisbett, 2009.

128 Cahan & Cohen, 1989; Stelzl, Merz, Ehlers, & Remer, 1995.

129 The effect of schooling on intelligence initially suggests that it would be beneficial to enroll a child in school as early as possible. Ironically, this may not be the case. Often what determines whether a child succeeds is not how smart they are, but how smart they are relative to their classmates. While a child who starts school later will be less intelligent, their greater maturity means that they will be relatively

smarter than their classmates. This can give them an advantage when they are being ranked relative to their classmates to determine their academic standing. Therefore, it may be best to withhold a child from starting school early, but try and give them stimulation that is as close as possible to the stimulation they will receive once school begins.

130 De Groot, 1951.

131 Sherman & Key, 1932.

132 Flynn, 1987.

133 Flynn, 1999.

134 Mackintosh, 1998; Teasdale & Owen, 1987; Williams, 1998.

135 Greenfield, 1998.

136 Sheldon, 1940.

137 See also Howard, 2001.

138 Shaw et al. (2006, p. 676) states that "More intelligent children demonstrate a particularly plastic cortex, with an initial accelerated and prolonged phase of cortical increase, which yields to equally vigorous cortical thinning by early adolescence."

139 These examples are often referred to as declarative memory (Manns & Eichenbaum, 2006).

140 Corkin, 2002; Scoville & Milner, 1957.

141 Anterograde amnesia has been popularized by movies such as *Memento* and, less accurately, *50 first dates*.

142 There has been a lively debate as to whether it is the hippocampus itself that is critical for memory, or other nearby regions with similar connectivity that were also removed when HM was operated on (Lipton & Eichenbaum, 2008; Morris, 2007). This debate is not relevant for the current discussion as we are concerned with the mechanics of memory, not its exact location in the brain.

143 Martinez & Derrick, 1996.

144 Günther, 1982; McLeod, Plunkett & Rolls, 1998; Norman & O'Reilly, 2003; Rizzuto & Kahana, 2001.

145 Hawkins & Blakeslee, 2004.

146 Nettelbeck, 1999.

147 Ericsson, Krampe, & Tesch-Romer, 1993.

148 Miller, 1999.

149 Levi & Newborn, 2009.

150 Young, 2009.

151 The other information is still available to our auto-associative network, as it receives inputs from all areas of the cortex. This allows us to still identify different voices even when the same phoneme is being pronounced.

152 Of course, this is likely to be one of the reasons why programming computers to do speech perception has been so difficult. If we are not aware ourselves of how our brain makes these perceptions, how can we program this ability into computers?

153 Supporting this, it is found that infants can be more sensitive to differences in sounds than adults, as adults place sounds in categories by ignoring differences (Polka & Werker, 1994). For instance, unlike English speakers, native Japanese adults cannot discriminate between the "r" and "l" phonemes. This is because the "r" and "l" phonemes are not different phonemes in the Japanese language. On the other hand, Japanese infants can discriminate between these phonemes. It is sometimes claimed that adults can learn phonemes that are not a part of their native language, but this is likely due to perceptual learning rather than abstraction. In other words, adults learn to distinguish between the sounds, but they are not sensitive to the key features that define the sounds. Hence, someone who learns to discriminate between the sounds in adulthood would still be poor at generalizing their learning to new situations, such as when a different speaker is using the sound.

154 Interestingly, we don't actually need to have a computer be able to change its wiring. Once the appropriate connections have been determined (such as by having a computer learn by simulation initially), these appropriate connections could be hardwired in silicon. Then, each computer that was produced would not need to go through the learning process that human children do. It would possess adult intelligence from its initial activation.

155 Petzold, 2008.

156 Churchland & Sejnowski, 1992; Sejnowski, 2006.

157 It is sometimes claimed that problem solving can also be unconscious. You might be trying to work out the solution to a problem for hours without success. However, if you "sleep on it," you find that the solution comes to you quickly the next day. One contributing factor here is that when you are continually thinking about a problem, certain elements can get activated that you think are the solution but are not. The activation of these elements prevents your auto-associative network from retrieving the correct solution. By leaving the problem, your brain can reset and look at the problem anew. Since the incorrect elements are no longer activated, your auto-associative network can then more easily retrieve the correct solution (Anderson, 1990).

158 Blackmore, 2004; Crick, 1994; Edelman & Tononi, 2000.

159 Carlson, 2009; Sacks, 1985.

160 Hertz, 1995.

161 Ericsson & Delaney, 1999.

162 Hebb, 1949.

163 Farah, 2000.

164 Gaillard et al., 2009; Hebb, 1949; Srinivasan, Russell, Edelman & Tononi, 1999; Uhlhaas et al., 2009.

165 Berardi, Pizzorusso & Maffei, 2000; Kandel & Jessel, 1991; Knudsen, 1999.

166 Kaufman & Lichtenberger, 2000.

167 Curtis, 1977; Shattuck, 1980.

168 Johnson & Newport, 1989.

169 Doupe & Kuhl, 1999; Grimshaw, Adelstein, Bryden & MacKinnon, 1998; Mayberry & Lock, 2003; Newman, Bavelier, Corina, Jezzard & Neville, 2002; Pinker, 1994; Stromswold, 2000.

170 DeKeyser, 2000.

171 Smith & Reio (2006, p. 128) noted that "Although more literacy program participants achieved a GED [high school equivalency diploma] than did control group members who received no instruction, no statistically significant differences in literacy skills were found following participation, as measured by the Tests of Adult Literacy Skills." See also Friedlander & Martinson, 1996.

172 American Institutes for Research, 2006; Friedlander & Martinson, 1996.

173 Remember that it was observed that many researchers do not appreciate how difficult understanding is. It is perhaps not surprising that this error is made. They come from a highly-select group—chosen based on their ability to understand. They also typically converse with other people from this same group. Their lack of recognition of the difficulty in understanding perhaps reflects an unawareness of the challenges that are faced by people who are not part of such a select group.

174 Knudsen, 1999.

175 Rakic, Bourgeois, & Goldman-Rakic, 1994.

176 Terman, 1919.

177 Shurkin, 1992.

178 Ericsson, Krampe, & Tesch-Romer, 1993.

179 Of course, this was not a true experiment where individuals were randomly assigned to groups that did or did not undertake so much practice, so the possibility that there is a talent factor that leads some individuals to practice more

cannot be completely discounted. Still, the data do strikingly indicate that it is not just talent and practice also plays a critical role in exceptional performance.

180 Carlson, 2009; Molinari, Leggio & Thaut, 2007.
181 Lehman, 1953.
182 Gladwell, 2008.
183 Gladwell, 2008, p. 55.
184 McBride, 1997.
185 Solomon, 1995.
186 Howe, 1999.
187 Wright, 1943.
188 Bernstein, 1973.
189 Howe, 1999.
190 Ceci, 1996; Greenfield, 1997; Sternberg, 2004.
191 Rushton & Jensen, 2005; Vernon, 1982.
192 Holloway, 1988; Stevenson et al., 1990.
193 Nisbett, 2009.
194 Heine et al., 2001.
195 Stevenson & Stigler, 1992.

REFERENCES

Abeles, M., Prut, Y., Bergman, H., & Vaadia, E. (1994). Synchronization in neuronal transmission and its importance for information processing. *Progress in Brain Research, 102*, 395-404.

Ackerman, P. L., Beier, M. E., & Boyle, M. O. (2005). Working memory and intelligence: The same or different constructs? *Psychological Bulletin, 131*, 30-60.

American Institutes for Research (2006). *A review of the literature in adult numeracy: Research and conceptual issues*. Washington, DC.

Anderson, J. R. (1990). *Cognitive psychology and its implications* (3rd ed.). New York: W. H. Freeman.

Antonini, A., & Stryker, M. P. (1993). Rapid remodeling of axonal arbors in the visual cortex. *Science, 260*, 1819-1821.

Bartholomew, D. J. (2004). *Measuring intelligence: Facts and fallacies*. Cambridge, England: Cambridge University Press.

Baumeister, A. A., & Bacharach, V. R. (1996). A critical analysis of the infant health and development program. *Intelligence, 23*, 79-104.

Berardi, N., Pizzorusso, T., & Maffei, L. (2000). Critical periods during sensory development. *Current Opinion in Neurobiology, 10*, 138-145.

Berlucchi, G. & Buchtel, H. A. (2009). Neuronal plasticity: Historical roots and evolution of meaning. *Experimental Brain Research, 192*, 307-319.

Bernstein, J. (1973). *Einstein*. Glasglow: Wm Collins Sons.

Beyerstein, B. L. (1999). Whence cometh the myth that we only use 10% of our brains? In S. D. Sala (Ed.), *Mind myths: Exploring popular assumptions about the mind and brain* (pp. 3-24). New York: John Wiley & Sons.

Bindu, P. N., & Dharmangadan, B. (2007). Psychological concomitants of mathematical creativity among young adults. *Psychological Studies, 52*, 210-215.

Binet, A., & Simon, T. (1916). *The development of intelligence in children: The Binet-Simon scale* (E. S. Kite, Trans.). Baltimore: Williams & Wilkins.

Bjorklund, D. F. (1997). The role of immaturity in human development. *Psychological Bulletin, 122,* 153-169.

Black, J. E., & Greenough, W. T. (1986). Induction of pattern in neural structure by experience: Implications for cognitive development. In M. E. Lamb, A. L. Brown, & B. Rogoff (Eds.), *Advances in Developmental Psychology: Vol. 4* (pp. 1-50). Hillsdale, NJ: Erlbaum.

Blackmore, S. (2004). *Consciousness: An introduction.* Oxford: Oxford University Press.

Bolles, R. C. (1993). *The story of psychology: A thematic history.* Pacific Grove, CA: Brooks/Cole Publishing.

Boomsma, D. I., Busjahn, A., & Peltonen, L. (2002). Classical twin studies and beyond. *Nature reviews: Genetics, 3,* 872-882.

Bouchard, T. J., Jr. (1997). IQ similarity in twins reared apart: Findings and responses to critics. In R. J. Sternberg & E. L. Grigorenko (Eds.), *Intelligence, heredity, and environment* (pp. 126-160). Cambridge, England: Cambridge University Press.

Bouchard, T. J., Jr. (in press). Genetic influence on human intelligence (Spearman's *g*): How much? *Annals of Human Biology.*

Bourgeois, J. -P., Goldman-Rakic, P. S., & Rakic, P. (2000). Formation, elimination, and stabilization of synapses in the primate cerebral cortex. In M. S. Gazzaniga (Ed.), *The new cognitive neurosciences* (2nd ed., pp. 45-53). Cambridge, MA: MIT Press.

Bradmetz, J. (1999). Precursors of formal thought: A longitudinal study. *British Journal of Developmental Psychology, 17,* 61-81.

Brody, N. (1992). *Intelligence* (2nd ed.). San Diego: Academic Press.

Buss, D. M. (1999). *Evolutionary psychology: The new science of the mind.* Boston: Allyn & Bacon.

Cahan, S., & Cohen, N. (1989). Age versus schooling effects on intelligence development. *Child Development, 60,* 1239-1249.

Calvin, W. H. (1995). Cortical columns, modules, and Hebbian cell assemblies. In M. A. Arbib (Ed.), *The handbook of brain theory and neural networks* (pp. 269-272). Cambridge, MA: MIT Press.

Carey, S. S. (2003). *A beginner's guide to scientific method* (3rd ed.). Belmont, CA: Wadsworth.

Carlson, N. R. (2009). *Physiology of behavior* (10th ed.). Boston: Allyn & Bacon.

Carroll, J. B. (1993). *Human cognitive abilities: A survey of factor-analytic studies.* Cambridge, England: Cambridge University Press.

Caruso, D. R., Taylor, J. J., & Detterman, D. K. (1982). Intelligence research and intelligent policy. In D. K. Detterman & R. J. Sternberg (Eds.), *How and how much can intelligence be increased* (pp. 45-65). Norwood, NJ: Ablex.

Cattell, R. B. (1987). *Intelligence: Its structure, growth and action.* Amsterdam: North Holland.

Ceci, S. J. (1991). How much does schooling influence general intelligence and its cognitive components? A reassessment of the evidence. *Developmental Psychology, 27,* 703-722.

Ceci, S. J. (1996). *On intelligence: A bioecological treatise on intellectual development.* Cambridge, MA: Harvard University Press.

Chabris, C. F., Steele, K. M., Bella, S. D., Peretz, I., Dunlop, T., Dawe, L. A., Humphrey, G. K., Shannon, R. A., Kirby, J. L., Jr., Olmstead, C. G., & Rauscher, F. H. (1999). Prelude or requiem for the "Mozart effect"? *Nature, 400,* 826-828.

Changeux, J.-P. (1985). *Neuronal man: The biology of mind.* New York: Oxford University Press.

Chimpanzee Sequencing and Analysis Consortium. (2005). Initial sequence of the chimpanzee genome and comparison with the human genome. *Nature, 437,* 69-87.

Churchland, P. S., & Sejnowski, T. J. (1992). *The computational brain.* Cambridge, MA: MIT Press.

Colom, R., Jung, R. E., & Haier, R. J. (2006). Finding the g-factor in brain structure using the method of correlated vectors. *Intelligence, 34,* 561-570.

Corballis, M. C. (1999). Are we in our right minds? in S. D. Sala (Ed.), *Mind myths: Exploring popular assumptions about the mind and brain* (pp. 25-41). New York: John Wiley & Sons.

Corkin, S. (2002). What's new with the amnesic patient H.M.? *Nature Reviews Neuroscience, 3,* 153-160.

Crick, F. (1994). *The astonishing hypothesis: The scientific search for the soul.* New York: Scribner.

Curtis, S. (1977). *Genie: A psycholinguistic study of a modern-day 'wild-child'.* New York: Academic Press.

Damasio, A. R. (1990). Category-related recognition defects as a clue to the neural substrates of knowledge. *Trends in Neurosciences, 13,* 95-98.

Dayhoff, J. E. (1990). *Neural network architectures: An introduction.* New York: Van Nostrand Reinhold.

De Groot, A. D. (1951). War and the intelligence of youth. *Journal of Abnormal and Social Psychology, 46,* 596-597.

Deacon, T. W. (1990). Rethinking mammalian brain evolution. *American Zoologist, 30,* 629-705.

Deary, I. J. (2000). *Looking down on human intelligence: From psychometrics to the brain.* Oxford, England: Oxford University Press.

Deary, I. J. (2003). Reaction time and psychometric intelligence: Jensen's contributions. In H. Nyborg (Ed.), *The scientific study of general intelligence: A tribute to Arthur R. Jensen* (pp. 53-75). Oxford: Pergamon.

DeKeyser, R. M. (2000). The robustness of the critical period in second language acquisition. *Studies in Second Language Acquisition, 22,* 499-533.

Detterman, D. K. (1994). Theoretical possibilities: The relation of human intelligence to basic cognitive abilities. In D. K. Detterman (Ed.), *Current topics in human intelligence: Vol. 4* (pp. 85-115). Norwood, NJ: Ablex.

Doupe, A. J., & Kuhl, P. K. (1999). Birdsong and human speech: Common themes and mechanisms. *Annual Review of Neuroscience, 22,* 567-631.

Duncan, J., Seitz, R. J., Kolodny, J., Bor, D., Herzog, H., Ahmed, A., Newell, F. N., & Emslie, H. (2000). A neural basis for general intelligence. *Science, 289,* 457-460.

Dunn, J., & Plomin, R. (1990). *Separate Lives: Why siblings are so different.* New York: Basic Books.

Edelman, G. M., & Tononi, G. (2000). *A universe of consciousness: How matter becomes imagination.* New York: Basic Books.

Elman, J. L., Bates, E. A., Johnson, M. H., Karmiloff-Smith, A., Parisi, D., & Plunkett, K. (1996). *Rethinking innateness: A connectionist perspective on development.* Cambridge, MA: MIT Press.

Erbas, E. A., Meinertzhagen, I. A., & Shaw, S. R. (1991). Evolution in nervous systems. *Annual Review of Neuroscience, 14,* 9-38.

Ericsson, K. A., & Delaney, P. F. (1999). Long-term working memory as an alternative to capacity models of working memory in everyday skilled performance. In A. Miyake & P. Shah (Eds.), *Models of working memory: Mechanisms of active maintenance and executive control* (pp. 257-297). Cambridge, England: Cambridge University Press.

Ericsson, K. A., Krampe, R. T., & Tesch-Romer, C. (1993). The role of deliberate practice in the acquisition of expert performance. *Psychological Review, 100,* 363-406.

Eriksson, P. S., Perfilieva, E., Björk-Eriksson, T., Alborn, A., Nordborg, C., Peterson, D. A., & Gage, F. H. (1998). Neurogenesis in the adult human hippocampus. *Nature Medicine, 4,* 1313-1317.

Erwin, E., Obermayer, K., & Schulten, K. (1995). Models of orientation and ocular dominance columns in the visual cortex: A critical comparison. *Neural Computa-*

tion, 7, 425-468.

Eysenck, H. J. (1994). A biological theory of intelligence. In D. K. Detterman (Ed.), *Current topics in human intelligence: Vol. 4* (pp. 117-149). Norwood, NJ: Ablex.

Eysenck, H. J., & Schoenthaler, S. J. (1997). Raising IQ level by vitamin and mineral supplementation. In R. J. Sternberg & E. L. Grigorenko (Eds.), *Intelligence, heredity, and environment* (pp. 363-392). Cambridge, England: Cambridge University Press.

Farah, M. J. (2000). The neural bases of mental imagery. In M. S. Gazzaniga (Ed.), *The new cognitive neurosciences* (2nd ed., pp. 965-974). Cambridge, MA: MIT Press.

Fine, l., Wade, A. R., Brewer, A. A., May, M. G., Goodman, D. F., Boynton, G. M., Wandell, B. A., MacLeod, D. I. A. (2003). Long-term deprivation affects visual perception and cortex. *Nature Neuroscience, 6,* 915-916.

Flavell, J. H. (1963). *The developmental psychology of Jean Piaget.* Princeton, NJ: Van Nostrand.

Flynn, J. R. (1987). Massive IQ gains in 14 nations: What IQ tests really measure. *Psychological Bulletin, 101,* 171-191.

Flynn, J. R. (1999). Searching for justice: The discovery of IQ gains over time. *American Psychologist, 54,* 5-20.

Friedlander, D., & Martinson, K. (1996). Effects of mandatory basic education for adult AFDC recipients. *Educational Evaluation and Policy Analysis, 18,* 327-337.

Fuster, J. M. (1995). Gradients of cortical plasticity. In J. L. McGaugh, N. M. Weinberger, & G. Lynch (Eds.), *Brain and memory: Modulation and mediation of neuroplasticity* (pp. 250-256). New York: Oxford University Press.

Gaillard, R., Dehaene, S., Adam, C., Clémenceau, S., Hasboun, D., Baulac, M., Cohen, L., & Nacchae, L. (2009). Converging intracranial markers of conscious access. *PLoS Biology, 7,* 472-492.

Gardner, H. (1993). *Frames of mind: The theory of multiple intelligences* (2nd ed.). New York: Basic Books.

Garlick, D. (2002). Understanding the nature of the general factor of intelligence: The role of individual differences in neural plasticity as an explanatory mechanism. *Psychological Review, 109,* 116-136.

Garlick, D. (2003). Integrating brain science research with intelligence research. *Current Directions in Psychological Science, 12,* 185-189.

Gierer, A., & Muller, C. M. (1995). Development of layers, maps and modules. *Current Opinion in Neurobiology, 5,* 91-97.

Gladwell, M. (2008). *Outliers: The story of success.* New York: Little Brown.

Goodman, R. A., & Whitaker, H. A. (1985). Hemispherectomy: A review (1928-1981) with special reference to the linguistic abilities and disabilities of the residual right hemisphere. In C. T. Best (Ed.), *Hemispheric function and collaboration in the child* (pp. 121-155). Orlando, FL: Academic Press.

Gottfredson, L. S. (1997). Mainstream science on intelligence: An editorial with 52 signatories, history, and bibliography. *Intelligence, 24,* 13-23.

Gottfredson, L. S. (2002). *g*: Highly general and highly practical. In R. J. Sternberg & E. L. Grigorenko (Eds.), *The general factor of intelligence: How general is it?* (pp. 331-380). Mahwah, NJ: Lawrence Erlbaum Associates.

Gould, E., Reeves, A. J., Fallah, M., Tanapat, P., Gross, C. G., & Fuchs, E. (1999). Hippocampal neurogenesis in adult Old World primates. *Proceedings of the National Academy of Sciences USA, 96,* 5263-5267.

Gould, S. J. (1977). *Onthogeny and phylogeny.* Cambridge, MA: Belknap Press.

Greenfield, P. M. (1997). You can't take it with you: Why ability assessments don't cross cultures. *American Psychologist, 52,* 1115-1124.

Greenfield, P. M. (1998). The cultural evolution of IQ. In U. Neisser (Ed.), *The rising curve: Long-term gains in IQ and related measures* (pp. 81-123). Washington, DC: American Psychological Association.

Greenough, W. T., Wallace, C. S., Alcantara, A. A., Anderson, B. J., Hawrylak, N., Sirevaag, A. M., Weiler, I. J., & Withers, G. S. (1993). Development of the brain: Experience affects the structure of neurons, glia, and blood vessels. In N. J. Anastasiow & S. Harel (Eds.), *At-risk infants: Interventions, families and research* (pp. 173-185). Baltimore: Paul H. Brookes.

Grimshaw, G. M., Adelstein, A., Bryden, M. P., & MacKinnon, G. E. (1998). First-language acquisition in adolescence: Evidence for a critical period for verbal language development. *Brain and Language, 63,* 237-255.

Günther, P. (1982). *Neural assemblies: An alternative approach to artificial intelligence.* New York: Springer Verlag.

Hata, Y., Ohshima, M., Ichisaka, S., Wakita, M., Fukuda, M., & Tsumoto, T. (2000). Brain-derived neurotrophic factor expands ocular dominance columns in visual cortex in monocularly deprived and nondeprived kittens but does not in adult cats. *Journal of Neuroscience, 20,* RC57, 1-5.

Haworth, C. M. A., Wright, M. J., Luciano, M., Martin, N. G., de Geus, E. J. C., van Beijsterveldt, C. E. M., et al. (in press). The heritability of general cognitive ability increases linearly from childhood to adulthood. *Molecular Psychiatry.*

Hawkins, J., & Blakeslee, S. (2004). *On intelligence.* New York: Times Books.

Hebb, D. O. (1949). *The organization of behavior: A neuropsychological theory.* New York:

John Wiley.

Heine, S. J., Kitayama, S., Lehman, D. R., Takata, T., Ide, E., Leung, C., & Matsumoto, H. (2001). Divergent consequences of success and failure in Japan and North America: An investigation of self-improving motivation. *Journal of Personality and Social Psychology, 81*, 599-615.

Hensch, T. K. (2004). Critical period regulation. *Annual Review of Neuroscience, 27*, 549-579.

Herrnstein, R. J., & Murray, C. (1994). *The bell curve: Intelligence and class structure in American life*. New York: Free Press.

Hertz, J. (1995). Sensory coding and information theory. In M. A. Arbib (Ed.), *The handbook of brain theory and neural networks* (pp. 864-867). Cambridge, MA: MIT Press.

Hirsch, H. V. B., & Spinelli, D. N. (1971). Modification of the distribution of receptive field orientations in cats by selective visual exposure during development. *Experimental Brain Research, 12*, 509-527.

Holloway, S. (1988). Concepts of ability and effort in Japan and the United States. *Review of Educational Research, 58*, 327-345.

Horn, J. (1998). A basis for research on age differences in cognitive capabilities. In J. J. McArdle & R. W. Woodcock (Eds.), *Human cognitive abilities in theory and practice* (pp. 57-91). Chicago: Riverside.

Howard, R. W. (2001). Searching the real world for signs of rising population intelligence. *Personality and Individual Differences, 30*, 1039-1058.

Howe, M. J. A. (1999). *Genius explained*. Cambridge, England: Cambridge University Press.

Hubel, D. H., & Wiesel, T. N. (1979). Brain mechanisms of vision. *Scientific American, 241(3)*, 130-144.

Hunt, R. R., & Worthen, J. B. (Eds.) (2006). *Distinctiveness and memory*. New York: Oxford University Press.

Huttenlocher, P. R. (1990). Morphometric study of human cerebral cortex development. *Neuropsychologia, 28*, 517-527.

Huttenlocher, P. R., & Dabholkar, A. S. (1997). Regional differences in synaptogenesis in human cerebral cortex. *Journal of Comparative Neurology, 387*, 167-178.

International Human Genome Sequencing Consortium. (2004). Finishing the euchromatic sequence of the human genome. *Nature, 431*, 931-945.

Jaeggi, S. M., Buschkuehl, M., Jonides, J., & Perrig, W. J. (2008). Improving fluid intelligence with training on working memory. *Proceedings of the National Academy of*

Sciences USA, 105, 6829-6833.

Jensen, A. R. (1969). How much can we boost IQ and scholastic achievement? *Harvard Educational Review, 39,* 1-123.

Jensen, A. R. (1980). *Bias in mental testing.* New York: Free Press.

Jensen, A. R. (1998). *The g factor: The science of mental ability.* Westport, CT: Praeger.

Jensen, A. R. (2006). *Clocking the mind: Mental chronometry and individual differences.* Amsterdam: Elsevier.

Johnson, J. S., & Newport, E. L. (1989). Critical period effects in second language learning: The influence of maturational state on the acquisition of English as a second language. *Cognitive Psychology, 21,* 60-99.

Johnson, W., Turkheimer, E., Gottesman, I. I., & Bouchard, T. J., Jr. (2009). Beyond heritability: Twin studies in behavioral research. *Current Directions in Psychological Science, 18,* 217-220.

Johnston, M. V., Ishida, A., Ishida, W. N., Matsushita, H. B., Nishimura, A., & Tsuji, M. (2009). Plasticity and injury in the developing brain. *Brain and Development, 31,* 1-10.

Kalat, J. W. (2007). *Biological psychology* (9th ed.). Belmont, CA: Thomson Wadsworth.

Kandel, E. R., & Jessell, T. (1991). Early experience and the fine tuning of synaptic connections. In E. R. Kandel, J. H. Schwartz, & T. M. Jessell (Eds.), *Principles of neural science* (3rd ed., pp. 945-958). London: Prentice-Hall.

Kane, M. J., & Engle, R. W. (2002). The role of prefrontal cortex in working-memory capacity, executive attention, and general fluid intelligence: An individual-differences perspective. *Psychonomic Bulletin and Review, 9,* 637-671.

Karnath, H., Milner, A. D., & Vallar, G. (2002). *The cognitive and neural bases of spatial neglect.* Oxford: Oxford University Press.

Kaufman, A. S., & Lichtenberger, E. O. (2000). *Essentials of WISC-III and WPPSI-R assessment.* New York: Wiley.

Kaufman, A. S., & Lichtenberger, E. O. (2006). *Assessing adolescent and adult intelligence* (3rd ed.). Hoboken, NJ: John Wiley & Sons.

Knudsen, E. I. (1999). Early experience and critical periods. In M. J. Zigmond, F. E. Bloom, S. C. Landis, J. L. Roberts, & L. R. Squire (Eds.), *Fundamental neuroscience* (pp. 637-654). San Diego: Academic Press.

Kritzer, M. F., & Goldman-Rakic, P. S. (1995). Intrinsic circuit organization of the major layers and sublayers of the dorsolateral prefrontal cortex in the rhesus monkey. *Journal of Comparative Neurology, 359,* 131-143.

Kyllonen, P. C., & Christal, R. E. (1990). Reasoning ability is (little more than) working-memory capacity?! *Intelligence, 14,* 389-433.

Lehman, H. C. (1953). *Age and achievement.* Princeton, NJ: Princeton University.

Levi, D., & Newborn, M. (2009). *How computers play chess.* San Rafael, CA: Ishi press.

Levitt, P. (2000). Molecular determinants of regionalization of the forebrain and cerebral cortex. In M. S. Gazzaniga (Ed.), *The new cognitive neurosciences* (2nd ed., pp. 23-32). Cambridge, MA: MIT Press.

Lipton, P. A., & Eichenbaum, H. (2008). Complementary roles of hippocampus and medial entorhinal cortex in episodic memory. *Neural Plasticity, 2008,* 1-8.

Loehlin, J. C., Horn, J. M., & Willerman, L. (1997). Heredity, environment, and IQ in the Texas adoption project. In R. J. Sternberg & E. L. Grigorenko (Eds.), *Intelligence, heredity, and environment* (pp. 105-125). Cambridge, England: Cambridge University Press.

Luria, A. R. (1966). *Higher cortical functions in man.* London: Tavistock.

Mackintosh, N. J. (1986). The biology of intelligence? *British Journal of Psychology, 77,* 1-18.

Mackintosh, N. J. (1998). *IQ and human intelligence.* Oxford, England: Oxford University Press.

Manns, J. R., & Eichenbaum, H. (2006). Evolution of declarative memory. *Hippocampus, 16,* 795-808.

Martin, A., Ungerleider, L. G., & Haxby, J. V. (2000). Category specificity and the brain: The sensory/motor model of semantic representations of objects. In M. S. Gazzaniga (Ed.), *The new cognitive neurosciences* (2nd ed., pp. 1023-1036). Cambridge, MA: MIT Press.

Martinez, J. L., Jr., & Derrick, B. E. (1996). Long-term potentiation and learning. *Annual Review of Psychology, 47,* 173-203.

Mayberry, R. I., & Lock, E. (2003). Age constraints on first versus second language acquisition: Evidence for linguisitic plasticity and epigenesis. *Brain and Language, 87,* 369-384.

Mayes, S. D., Calhoun, S. L., Bixler, E. O., & Zimmerman, D. N. (2009). IQ and neuropsychological predictors of academic achievement. *Learning and Individual Differences, 19,* 238-241.

McBride, J. (1997). *Steven Spielberg: A biography.* New York: Simon & Schuster.

McDaniel, M. A. (2005). Big-brained people are smarter: A meta-analysis of the relationship between in vivo brain volume and intelligence. *Intelligence, 33,* 337-346.

McLeod, P., Plunkett, K., & Rolls, E. T. (1998). *Introduction to connectionist modelling of cognitive processes.* Oxford, England: Oxford University Press.

Miller, L. K. (1999). The savant syndrome: Intellectual impairment and exceptional skill. *Psychological Bulletin, 125,* 31-46.

Miller, P. H. (1993). *Theories of developmental psychology* (3rd ed.). New York: W. H. Freeman and Company

Moffitt, T. E., Caspi, A., Harkness, A. R., & Silva, P. A. (1993). The natural history of change in intellectual performance: Who changes? How much? Is it meaningful? *Journal of Child Psychology and Psychiatry, 34,* 455-506.

Molinari, M., Leggio, M. G., & Thaut, M. H. (2007). The cerebellum and neural networks for rhythmic sensorimotor synchronization in the human brain. *The Cerebellum, 6,* 18-23.

Moody, D. E. (2009). Can intelligence be increased by training on a task of working memory? *Intelligence, 37,* 327-328.

Morris, R. (2007). Theories of hippocampal function. In P. Andersen, R. Morris, D. Amaral, T. Bliss, & J. O'Keefe (Eds.), *The hippocampus book* (pp. 581-714). New York: Oxford University Press.

Morrison, J. H., & Hof, P. R. (1997). Life and death of neurons in the aging brain. *Science, 278,* 412-419.

Mountcastle, V. B. (1998). *Perceptual neuroscience: The cerebral cortex.* Cambridge, MA: Harvard University Press.

Mrzljak, L., Uylings, H. B. M., Van Eden, C. G., & Judas, M. (1990). Neuronal development in human prefrontal cortex in prenatal and postnatal stages. *Progress in Brain Research, 85,* 185-222.

Muter, V., Taylor, S., & Vargha-Khadem, F. (1997). A longitudinal study of early intellectual development in hemiplegic children. *Neuropsychologia, 35,* 289-298.

Navon, D. (1984). Resources—A theoretical soup stone? *Psychological Review, 91,* 216-234.

Neisser, U., Boodoo, G., Bouchard, T. J., Jr., Boykin, A. W., Brody, N., Ceci, S. J., Halpern, D. F., Loehlin, J. C., Perloff, R., Sternberg, R. J., & Urbina, S. (1996). Intelligence: Knowns and unknowns. *American Psychologist, 51,* 77-101.

Nettelbeck, T. (1999). Savant syndrome—Rhyme without reason. In M. Anderson (Ed.), *The development of intelligence* (pp. 247-273). East Sussex, United Kingdom: Psychology Press.

Newman, A. J., Bavelier, D., Corina, D., Jezzard, P., & Neville, H. J. (2002). A critical period for right hemisphere in American Sign Language processing. *Nature Neuroscience, 5,* 76-80.

Nisbett, R. E. (2009). *Intelligence and how to get it: Why schools and cultures count.* New York: Norton.

Norman, K. A., & O'Reilly, R. C. (2003). Modeling hippocampal and neocortical contributions to recognition memory: A complementary learning systems approach. *Psychological Review, 110*, 611-646.

O'Donnell, S., Noseworthy, M. D., Levine, B., & Dennis, M. (2005). Cortical thickness of the frontopolar area in typically developing children and adolescents. *Neuroimage, 24*, 948-954.

O'Leary, D. D. M. (1996). Areal specialization of the developing neocortex: Differentiation, developmental plasticity and genetic specification. In D. Magnusson (Ed.), *The lifespan development of individuals: Behavioral, neurobiological, and psychosocial perspectives: A synthesis* (pp. 23-37). Cambridge, England: Cambridge University Press.

Oppenheim, J. S., Skerry, J. E., Tramo, M. J., & Gazzaniga, M. S. (1989). Magnetic resonance imaging morphology of the corpus callosum in monozygotic twins. *Annals of Neurology, 26*, 100-104.

O'Reilly, R. C., & Munakata, Y. (2000). *Computational explorations in cognitive neuroscience: Understanding the mind by simulating the brain.* Cambridge, MA: Bradford.

Ostrovsky, Y., Meyers, E., Ganesh, S., Mathur, U., & Sinha, P. (in press). Visual parsing after recovery from blindness. *Psychological Science.*

Park, G., Lubinski, D., & Benbow, C. P. (2008). Ability differences among people who have commensurate degrees matter for scientific creativity. *Psychological Science, 19*, 957-961.

Pettigrew, J. D., & Freeman, R. D. (1973). Visual experience without lines: Effect on developing cortical neurons. *Science, 182*, 599-601.

Petzold, C. (2009). *The annotated Turing: A guided tour through Alan Turing's historic paper on computability and the Turing machine.* Indianapolis, IN: Wiley.

Piaget, J. (1952). *The origins of intelligence in children.* New York: International Universities Press.

Pinel, J. P. J. (2007). *Basics of biopsychology.* Boston: Allyn & Bacon.

Pinker, S. (1994). *The language instinct.* New York: William Morrow.

Plomin, R. (1990). *Nature and nurture: An introduction to human behavioral genetics.* Pacific Grove, CA: Brooks/Cole.

Plomin, R. (1999). Genetic research on general cognitive ability as a model for mild mental retardation. *International Review of Psychiatry, 11*, 34-46.

Pol, H. E. H., Schnack, H. G., Posthuma, D., Mandl, R. C. W., Baaré, W. F., van Oel, C., van Haren, N. E., Collins, D. L., Evans, A. C., Amunts, K., Bürgel, U., Zilles, K., de Geus, E., Boomsma, D. I., & Kahn, R. S. (2004). Genetic contributions to human brain morphology and intelligence. *The Journal of Neuroscience, 26*, 10235-10242.

Poldrack, R. A. (2000). Imaging brain plasticity: Conceptual and methodological issues—A theoretical review. *Neuroimage, 12*, 1-13.

Polka, L., & Werker, J. F. (1994). Developmental changes in perception of nonnative vowel contrasts. *Journal of Experimental Psychology: Human Perception and Performance, 20*, 421-435.

Polleux, F. (2005). Genetic mechanisms specifying cortical connectivity: Let's make some projections together. *Neuron, 46*, 395-400.

Preuss, T. M. (2000). What's human about the human brain? In M. S. Gazzaniga (Ed.), *The new cognitive neurosciences* (2nd ed., pp. 1219-1234). Cambridge, MA: MIT Press.

Price, D. J., Lotto, R. B., Warren, N., Magowan, G., & Clausen, J. (1995). The roles of growth factors and neural activity in the development of the neocortex. In G. R. Bock & G. Cardew (Eds.), *Development of the cerebral cortex* (pp. 231-250). Chichester: John Wiley & Sons.

Rakic, P. (1995). Corticogenesis in human and nonhuman primates. In M. S. Gazzaniga (Ed.), *The cognitive neurosciences* (pp. 127-145). Cambridge, MA: MIT Press.

Rakic, P., Bourgeois, J. -P., & Goldman-Rakic, P. S. (1994). Synaptic development of the cerebral cortex: Implications for learning, memory, and mental illness. *Progress in Brain Research, 102*, 227-243.

Rijsdijk, F. V., Boomsma, D. I., & Vernon, P. A. (1995). Genetic analysis of peripheral nerve conduction velocity in twins. *Behavior Genetics, 25*, 341-348.

Rizzuto, D. S., & Kahana, M. J. (2001). An autoassociative neural network model of paired associate learning. *Neural Computation, 13*, 2075-2092.

Roder, B., Rosler, F., & Neville, H. J. (2000). Event-related potentials during auditory language processing in congenitally blind and sighted people. *Neuropsychologia, 38*, 1482-1502.

Roth, E. A., & Smith, K. H. (2008). The Mozart effect: Evidence for the arousal hypothesis. *Perceptual and Motor Skills, 107*, 396-402.

Rovee-Collier, C. (1999). The development of infant memory. *Current Directions in Psychological Science, 8(3)*, 80-85.

Rumelhart, D. E., & McClelland, J. L. (Eds.) (1986). *Parallel distributed processing: Explorations in the microstructure of cognition. Volume 1: Foundations.* Cambridge, MA: MIT Press.

Rushton, J. P., & Jensen, A. R. (2005). Thirty years of research on race differences in cognitive ability. *Psychology, Public Policy, and Law, 11*, 235-294.

Sacks, O. W. (1985). *The man who mistook his wife for a hat and other clinical tales*. New York: Summit Books.

Schmidt, F. L., & Hunter, J. E. (2004). General mental ability in the world of work: Occupational attainment and job performance. *Journal of Personality and Social Psychology, 86*, 162-173.

Scoville, W. B., & Milner, B. (1957). Loss of recent memory after bilateral hippocampal lesions. *Journal of Neurology, Neurosurgery and Psychiatry, 20*, 11-21.

Seitz, A. R., & Dinse, H. R. (2007). A common framework for perceptual learning. *Current Opinion in Neurobiology, 17*, 148-153.

Sejnowski, T. J. (2006). What are the projective fields of cortical neurons? In J. L. van Hemmen & T. J. Sejnowski (Eds.), *23 problems in systems neuroscience* (pp. 394-405). New York: Oxford University Press.

Sharma, A., Nash, A. A., & Dorman, M. (2009). Cortical development, plasticity and re-organization in children with cochlear implants. *Journal of Communication Disorders, 42*, 272-279.

Shattuck, R. (1980). *The forbidden experiment: The story of the Wild Boy of Aveyron*. New York: Farrar Straus Giroux.

Shaw, P., Greenstein, D., Lerch, J., Clasen, L., Lenroot, R., Gogtay, N., Evans, A., Rapoport, J., & Giedd, J. (2006). Intellectual ability and cortical development in children and adolescents. *Nature, 440*, 676-679.

Sheldon, W. H. (1940). *The varieties of human physique: An introduction to constitutional psychology*. New York: Harper & Brothers.

Sheppard, L. D., & Vernon, P. A. (2008). Intelligence and speed of information-processing: A review of 50 years of research. *Personality and Individual Differences, 44*, 535-551.

Sherman, M., & Key, C. B. (1932). The intelligence of isolated mountain children. *Child Development, 3*, 279-290.

Shurkin, J. N. (1992). *Terman's kids: The groundbreaking study of how the gifted grow up*. New York: Little Brown.

Singer, W. (1995). Development and plasticity of cortical processing architectures. *Science, 270*, 758-764.

Skoyles, J. R. (1999). Human evolution expanded brains to increase expertise capacity, not IQ. *Psycoloquy, 10:002*.

Smith, M. C., & Reio, T. G. Jr. (2006). Adult development, schooling, and the transition to work. In P. A. Alexander & P. H. Winne (Eds.), *Handbook of educational psychology* (2nd ed., pp. 115-138). Mahwah, NJ: Lawrence Erlbaum.

Snow, R. E. (1995). Pygmalion and intelligence. *Current Directions in Psychological*

Science, 4, 169-171.

Snyderman, M., & Rothman, S. (1987). Survey of expert opinion on intelligence and aptitude testing. *American Psychologist, 42,* 137-144.

Solomon, M. (1996). *Mozart: A life.* New York: HarperCollins.

Spearman, C. (1904). General intelligence, objectively determined and measured. *American Journal of Psychology, 15,* 201-293.

Spitz, H. H. (1999). Attempts to raise intelligence. In M. Anderson (Ed.), *The development of intelligence* (pp. 275-293). East Sussex, UK: Psychology Press.

Squire, L. R. (2004). Memory systems of the brain: A brief history and current perspective. *Neurobiology of Learning and Memory, 82,* 171-177.

Srinivasan, R., Russell, D. P., Edelman, G. M., & Tononi, G. (1999). Increased synchronization of neuromagnetic responses during conscious perception. *Journal of Neuroscience, 19,* 5435-5448.

Stelzl, I., Merz, F., Ehlers, T., & Remer, H. (1995). The effect of schooling on the development of fluid and crystallized intelligence: A quasi-experimental study. *Intelligence, 21,* 279-296.

Sternberg, R. J. (1985). *Beyond IQ: A triarchic theory of intelligence.* New York: Cambridge University Press.

Sternberg, R. J. (2004). Culture and intelligence. *American Psychologist, 59,* 325-338.

Stevenson, H. W., & Stigler, J. W. (1992). *The learning gap: Why our schools are failing and what can we learn from Japanese and Chinese education.* New York: Summit books.

Stevenson, H. W., Lee, S. Y., Chen, C., Stigler, J. W., Hsu, C. C., & Kitamura, S. (1990). Contexts of achievement: A study of American, Chinese and Japanese children. *Monographs for the Society for Research in Child Development, 55 (1-2),* 1-123.

Stirling, J. (2000). *Cortical functions.* London: Routledge.

Streissguth, A. P., Barr, H. M., Sampson, P. D., Darby, B. L., & Martin, D. C. (1989). IQ at age 4 in relation to maternal alcohol use and smoking during pregnancy. *Developmental Psychology, 25,* 3-11.

Stromswold, K. (2000). The cognitive neuroscience of language acquisition. In M. S. Gazzaniga (Ed.), *The new cognitive neurosciences* (2nd ed., pp. 909-932). Cambridge, MA: MIT Press.

Swindale, N. V. (1996). The development of topography in the visual cortex: A review of models. *Network: Computation in Neural Systems, 7,* 161-247.

Teasdale, T. W., & Owen, D. R. (1987). National secular trends in intelligence and education: A twenty-year cross-sectional study. *Nature, 325,* 119-121.

Terman, L. M. (1919). *The measurement of intelligence.* London: George G. Harrap.

Thompson, W. F., Schellenberg, E. G., & Husain, G. (2001). Arousal, mood, and the Mozart Effect. *Psychological Science, 12,* 248-251.

Tierney, M. C., Varga, M., Hosey, L., Grafman, J., & Braun, A. (2001). PET evaluation of bilingual language compensation following early childhood brain damage. *Neuropsychologia, 39,* 114-121.

Tooby, J., & Cosmides, L. (1995). Mapping the evolved functional organization of mind and brain. In M. S. Gazzaniga (Ed.), *The cognitive neurosciences* (pp. 1185-1197). Cambridge, MA: MIT Press.

Uhlhaas, P. J., Pipa, G., Lima, B., Melloni, L., Neuenschwander, S., Nikolic, D., Singer, W. (2009). Neural synchrony in cortical networks: History, concept and current status. *Frontiers in Integrative Neuroscience, 3,* ArtID 17.

Uylings, H. B. M. (2006). Development of the human cortex and the concept of "critical" or "sensitive" periods. *Language Learning, 56(Suppl 1),* 59-90.

Uylings, H. B. M., Van Pelt, J., Parnavelas, J. G., & Ruiz-Marcos, A. (1994). Geometrical and topological characteristics in the dendritic development of cortical pyramidal and non-pyramidal neurons. *Progress in Brain Research, 102,* 109-123.

Valvo, A. (1971). *Sight restoration after long-term blindness: The problems and behavior patterns of visual rehabilitation.* New York: American Foundation for the Blind.

Van Veen, M. P., & Van Pelt, J. (1994). Dynamic mechanisms of neuronal outgrowth. *Progress in Brain Research, 102,* 95-108.

Vernon, P. E. (1982). *The abilities and achievements of Orientals in North America.* New York: Academic Press.

Vicari, S., Albertoni, A., Chilosi, A. M., Cipriani, P., Cioni, G., & Bates, E. (2000). Plasticity and reorganization during language development in children with early brain injury. *Cortex, 36,* 31-46.

Wechsler, D. (1944). *The measurement of adult intelligence* (3rd ed.). Baltimore: Williams & Wilkins.

Wickett, J. C., & Vernon, P. A. (1994). Peripheral nerve conduction velocity, reaction time, and intelligence: An attempt to replicate Vernon and Mori (1992). *Intelligence, 18,* 127-131.

Wickett, J. C., Vernon, P. A., & Lee, D. H. (2000). Relationships between factors of intelligence and brain volume. *Personality and Individual Differences, 29,* 1095-1122.

Williams, R. W., & Herrup, K. (1988). The control of neuron number. *Annual Review of Neuroscience, 11,* 423-453.

Williams, W. M. (1998). Are we raising smarter children today? School—and home-related influences on IQ. In U. Neisser (Ed.), *The rising curve: Long-term gains in IQ and related measures* (pp. 125-154). Washington, DC: American Psychological Association.

Wilson, E. O. (1975). *Sociobiology: The new synthesis*. Cambridge, MA: Harvard University Press.

Wilson, R. S. (1983). The Louisville twin study: Developmental synchronies in behavior. *Child Development, 54*, 298-316.

Wiskott, L., Rasch, M. J., & Kempermann, G. (2006). A functional hypothesis for adult hippocampal neurogenesis: Avoidance of catastrophic interference in the dentate gyrus. *Hippocampus, 16*, 329-343.

Wright, F. L. (1943). *An autobiography*. New York: Duell, Sloan & Pearce.

Young, R. (2009). *How computers work: Processor and main memory*. Los Angeles, CA: Createspace.

Zhou, R., & Black, I. B. (2000). Development of neural maps: Molecular mechanisms. In M. S. Gazzaniga (Ed.), *The new cognitive neurosciences* (2nd ed., pp. 213-221). Cambridge, MA: MIT Press.